CIVILIZATIONS
FACTFINDER

Authors
Anita Ganeri, Hazel Mary Martell, Brian Williams

Editor
Jane Walker

Design
First Edition

Image Coordination
Ian Paulyn

Production Assistant
Jenni Cozens

Index
Jane Parker

Editorial Director
Paula Borton

Design Director
Clare Sleven

Publishing Director
Jim Miles

This edition published by Dempsey Parr, 1999
Dempsey Parr, Queen Street House, 4 Queen Street, Bath, BA1 1HE, UK

2 4 6 8 10 9 7 5 3 1

Produced by Miles Kelly Publishing Ltd
Bardfield Centre, Great Bardfield, Essex CM7 4SL

ISBN 1-84084-519-8

Printed in Singapore

CIVILIZATIONS

FACTFINDER

DP

DEMPSEY
PARR

INTRODUCTION

Humans are visual creatures.
We rely on eyesight more than
any other sense—especially to find
out about the world around us from
words and pictures. Lists of facts and
descriptions of events may contain
concentrated knowledge, but adding
illustrations helps to bring the subject
alive. They encourage us to delve
further, appreciate, and enjoy, as well
as to retain the information.

The FACTFINDER series is packed with a huge variety of facts and figures. It also explains processes and events in an easy-to-understand way, with diagrams, photographs, and captions. Fact panels on each main page area contain information for ready reference. Each title is divided into sections that deal with a major aspect of the subject. So look and learn, read and remember— and return again and again.

CONTENTS

The Age of Discovery 108

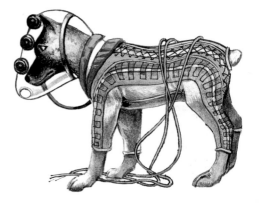

HISTORY OF THE WORLD

What is history? In its broadest sense, it is the study of our past—the story of people. Some historians look at important events such as wars, revolutions, changes of government and great inventions. Others are interested in the daily lives and routines of ordinary people.

The American industrialist Henry Ford once said that "History is bunk," but most people would disagree. Our lives today are shaped by the decisions and

actions of people decades and centuries ago. Another famous saying is that "History repeats itself."
By understanding the past, we may gain a more balanced view of the present, and make thoughtful plans for the future.

The basic aims of history are to record and explain our past. Historians study a range of written, pictorial and oral (spoken) evidence. This is a fascinating topic in itself, since people often recorded, not the facts, but what they wanted others to know.

This range of evidence is combined with archaeology, the study of things that people have left behind—from huge buildings to clay pots—to build up a picture of the past.

DISCOVERING THE PAST

The first people to study history seriously were the ancient Greeks. In the fifth century B.C., the Greek historian Herodotus set out to write a true and systematic record of the wars between the Greeks and the Persians. He hoped to preserve the memory of past events and show how two peoples came into conflict.

The study of archaeology, however, is a much more recent development. True archaeological investigation only began in the eighteenth century. Archaeologists today try to preserve even the tiniest fragments left behind by our ancestors, to help create a more complete picture of the past.

Interpreting the evidence is the most fascinating part of an historian's or archaeologist's job. Historians, however, must always be aware of bias or prejudice in the things that they read or write. Bias means being influenced by a particular point of view, while prejudice means "judging before"—before you have all the facts. All accounts are an interpretation of the events, sometimes unknowingly. Histories written by the ancient Egyptians, for example, record and praise the deeds of their kings with little concern for accuracy or doubt.

When historians read a text, they must ask themselves what was the attitude of the writer to the people or events being described? How close was the writer to the event? These questions must also be asked of oral history, when people's memories fade and can become exaggerated or distorted over time. Historians themselves are influenced by the times they live in. Modern historians try to avoid applying the values and beliefs of the present to their interpretations of the past.

ARCHAEOLOGICAL EVIDENCE

Archaeology is the study of the physical remains of the past—everything from a priceless statue to a garbage heap. Archaeology can tell us about societies that existed before written records were made, as well as adding to our knowledge of literate societies. In the past, archaeologists were little better than treasure-seekers. Today, however, they use scientific methods to analyze their finds and build a picture of the past.

Archaeologists study objects (artifacts), features (buildings), and ecofacts (seeds or animal bones). Some artifacts such as pottery, glass and metal, survive well, although often broken into many fragments. Objects made of organic materials, such as wood, leather and fabric, rarely survive— they quickly rot away leaving little or no trace behind. Organic materials survive best in waterlogged conditions, such as rivers or bogs, in very dry, desertlike areas, or in freezing conditions.

By studying the remains of human skeletons, experts can tell how tall people were, how long they lived and what diseases they suffered. Burials often reveal much about the social structure of an ancient society as well as its beliefs. Remains such as animal bones and shells can tell us about people's diets, while seeds, pollen and insect remains can build up a picture of their environment. When archaeologists discover a site they want to examine, they set up an excavation, or dig. Most archaeologists today work on rescue digs, attempting to record a site before it is completely destroyed by our present-day "progress."

HISTORICAL EVIDENCE

Before historians can interpret the past, they must first establish the facts about the events they are studying. Historians look for evidence by researching a wide range of documents and records, called historical sources.

Primary sources are accounts written by the people actually involved in the event being studied, and include government and legal papers, wills, maps, business agreements, letters, and diaries. Historians read a wide range of texts, not just actual accounts of past events, but also texts that show the interests and beliefs of people in the past, such as prayer books. Historians also look for evidence from government census returns, and birth, death, and marriage registers. Possibly the most famous census ever carried out was the Domesday Book, compiled in 1086 by order of William the Conqueror, king of England. This was the first thorough survey of part of the British Isles, detailing who owned the land, who lived there, and how much it was worth.

Historians also look for secondary sources—studies of primary sources made at a later date. Secondary sources include such documents as newspaper reports, or the books of previous historians. Newspapers are an especially important resource for modern historians.

Oral history is also a vital source of information. For thousands of years people have passed on their history by word of mouth from generation to generation, as stories, songs, and poetry.

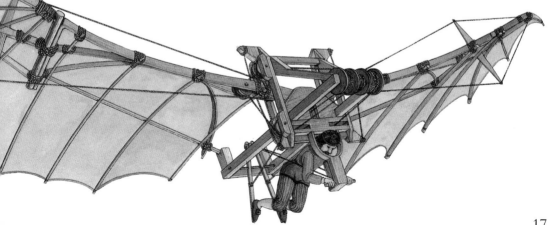

THE ANCIENT WORLD

4 million years ago to A.D. *500*

The period from about 4 million years ago to
A.D. 500 covers a vast sweep of the world's history,
from the appearance of the first human beings to
the fall of the Roman empire. Our earliest ancestors
appeared in Africa some 2.5 million years ago,
having evolved from apes who came down from
the trees and learned to walk upright on two
legs. Over thousands of years, they learned
how to make fire, hunt, and fashion tools.
The first ever metal tools and
weapons were made in the
Near East about 7,000 years
ago. Then, about 10,000 years ago, an
extraordinary change took place.

People learned how to grow crops and raise their own animals, rather than hunting and gathering. They began to build permanent homes, followed by towns and cities.

By about 5000 B.C., the world's first civilizations began to emerge along rivers where the land was rich for farming—Sumerians, Assyrians, Babylonians, then the ancient Egyptians, Greeks, and Romans. Civilizations flourished too in India, China, Persia, and in North and South America.

THE FIRST HUMANS

The first humanlike creatures appeared on our planet about 4 million years ago, in Africa. These "man-apes" came down from the trees and began to walk on two legs. The most complete man-ape skeleton was found in Ethiopia, East Africa, in 1974. Its scientific name was *Australopithecus* (meaning "southern ape"), but the skeleton was nicknamed "Lucy". The first true human beings, called *Homo habilis,* or "handy man", appeared about 2.5 million years ago. A million

FROM APE TO HUMAN
Early people gradually became less like apes and more like humans.

Southern ape

Handy man

Upright man

Neanderthal man

Modern man

AN EARLY TOOL

The hand ax was one of the earliest tools ever made. It was invented by Homo erectus *around 2 million years ago. Modern humans used hand axes until about 13,000 B.C.*

years later another species, *Homo erectus,* or "upright man," appeared. Early humans, or hominids, had bigger brains and were more intelligent than the man-apes. They learned to make tools, to hunt and gather food, to make shelters and fire, and to communicate. Modern humans, *Homo sapiens sapiens,* our direct ancestors, first lived about 100,000 years ago. By about 40,000 B.C., they had spread across Europe and had reached Australia.

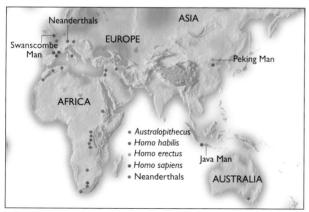

This map shows where important fossil remains of early people have been found.

c. 4 million years B.C. *Australopithecus* appear in Africa. They walk on two legs instead of on all fours.

c. 2.5–2 million years B.C. *Homo habilis* (handy man) appear in Africa. They are the first people to make tools.

c. 1.5 million years B.C. *Homo erectus* (upright man) appear in Africa. They were the first people to learn how to use fire.

c. 120,000 B.C. Neanderthal man appears in Africa, Asia, and Europe. They are the first humans to bury their dead.

c. 40,000 B.C. *Homo sapiens sapiens* (modern man) is now living in many parts of the world, including Australia.

c. 13,000 B.C. Modern humans cross from Asia into the Americas for the first time.

TOOLS AND ART

The first known tools were made from pebbles more than 2 million years ago. Gradually tools became more advanced. People discovered that flint was one of the best tool-making materials. It was very hard, and it could be chiseled into different shapes and sizes. Early people shaped flints into tools such as sharp-edged hand axes, knives, blades, scrapers, hatchets, and needles. Stone Age weapons included harpoons and sharp spearheads and arrowheads. These were made from flints, bones, and antlers. Bows and arrows, the earliest shooting weapons, were first used about 15,000 years ago.

Antler spearhead

Flint scraper

Flint fire lighter

Stone lamp and grinder

Antler chisel

Bone shuttle

PREPARING A HIDE

Stone Age people used stone blades to skin the animals they killed and scrape the hides clean. When the blade edges became blunt, they could easily be resharpened by chiseling. The prepared hides were used for making clothes, tents, and bags.

Pieces of hide were sewn together using needles made of antler or bone.

Peg holds skin.

CAVE ART

Some 40,000 years ago artists painted pictures of the animals they hunted on the walls of their cave shelters. Cave paintings have been found in Europe, Africa, Asia, and Australia. The most famous paintings in Europe are in the Lascaux Caves in southern France.

This bison painting was found in the Altamira Caves in Spain. It dates from about 12,000 B.C.

Knife blade to cut skin.

c. 2 million years–10,000 B.C. The Old Stone Age. First stone tools.

c. 40,000 B.C. Rock engravings in Australia.

c. 24,000 B.C. Cave paintings in Namibia, Africa.

c. 17,000 B.C. Cave paintings in France and Spain.

From c. 10,000 B.C. The Middle Stone Age. A greater variety of stone tools.

From c. 8000 B.C. The New Stone Age. Stone tools, such as sickles and hoes.

c. 5000 B.C. The Copper Age. People make metal tools and weapons for the very first time.

c. 3000 B.C. The Bronze Age begins in the Near East. Bronze is an alloy, or mixture, of copper and tin.

c. 1000 B.C. The Iron Age begins in Europe.

23

LIFE IN THE ICE AGES

About 24,000 years ago, temperatures across the world plummeted and the Earth was gripped by freezing, icy weather. A huge sheet of ice, more than 600 feet (180 m) thick in places, covered about a third of the Earth's surface. This is what we call the "Ice Age"—the last glacial period, which ended about 10,000 years ago. Experts think that ice ages are caused by changes in the path taken by the Earth as it orbits the Sun. Even the slightest difference can drastically affect the amount of heat reaching the Earth. As the seas froze over during the Ice Age, sea levels fell by more than 300 feet (90 m) in some places, exposing bridges of land between the continents. The Bering Strait between Siberia and Alaska became dry land,

creating a bridge between Asia and North America up to 600 miles (1,000 km) wide. The first people to reach North America probably walked across this land bridge.

Conditions were extremely harsh for the people who lived near the ice sheets. Woolly mammoths were a valuable source of meat, skins for clothes, and bones for weapons and carvings, but mammoth hunting was tough, dangerous work. The men hunted in groups, driving the mammoth into a corner or up against a cliff. Then they closed in for the kill, attacking the mammoth with sharp spears made of flint and wood and large stones. One mammoth could provide enough meat to feed a group for many months.

c. **2 million** B.C. The Quaternary ice age begins.

c. **22,000** B.C. The Ice Age enters its latest glacial. Ice covers about a third of the Earth.

c. **16,000** B.C. The last Ice Age reaches its coldest point. People living at Mezhirich in the Ukraine build huts from mammoth bones.

c. **13,000** B.C. Hunter-gatherers cross from Asia into North America via the now exposed Bering Strait.

c. **12,000** B.C. The Bering Strait floods over again, as the ice starts to melt and sea level rises.

c. **10,000** B.C. In Europe, the glaciers begin to retreat and the Ice Age ends.

c. **6000** B.C. Rising sea level separates Britain from the continent of Europe.

THE FIRST FARMERS

About 10,000 years ago, people learned how to grow crops, and to rear animals for their meat, milk, and skins. Instead of finding food by hunting wild animals and gathering nuts, berries, and roots, people found they could grow enough food on a small patch of land. They began to settle in one place and build permanent homes. They were the first farmers.

EARLY FARM LIFE
Life on a farm in Europe around 3000 B.C. was hard work. Farmers dug the ground with deer antlers. They planted seeds from wild plants and harvested the crops with stone sickles.

Farmers started to build permanent homes.

Stone axes were used to fell trees and clear ground.

The harvested grain was ground into flour for bread.

Clay storage pots   *Kiln*

CROPS AND FARM ANIMALS

Plants and animals that are grown or raised by people are known as domesticated. Wheat and barley were two of the first crops grown by farmers. These first domesticated plants were grown from seeds collected from wild plants. The crop was harvested and the grain used to make bread and beer. Farmers also learned how to tame and breed wild animals. The first domesticated animals were sheep, goats, and pigs.

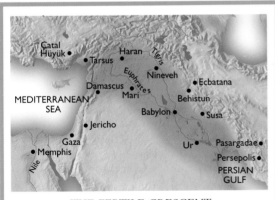

THE FERTILE CRESCENT

The first farms developed in the Near East and Europe in a region called the Fertile Crescent (shaded area). Many farming settlements became important towns.

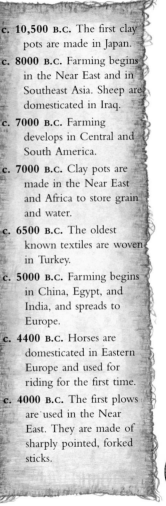

c. 10,500 B.C. The first clay pots are made in Japan.

c. 8000 B.C. Farming begins in the Near East and in Southeast Asia. Sheep are domesticated in Iraq.

c. 7000 B.C. Farming develops in Central and South America.

c. 7000 B.C. Clay pots are made in the Near East and Africa to store grain and water.

c. 6500 B.C. The oldest known textiles are woven in Turkey.

c. 5000 B.C. Farming begins in China, Egypt, and India, and spreads to Europe.

c. 4400 B.C. Horses are domesticated in Eastern Europe and used for riding for the first time.

c. 4000 B.C. The first plows are used in the Near East. They are made of sharply pointed, forked sticks.

27

THE FIRST TOWNS

As the world's population increased, towns grew up with a more complex way of life. Trade grew between the towns, as neighboring farmers bought and sold their surplus produce. The ruins of two ancient towns have provided archaeologists with a fascinating glimpse into the past—Jericho in Jordan, and Çatal Hüyük in Turkey. People have lived in the town of Jericho continuously since about 8000 B.C. to the present day. Its massive stone walls have been destroyed many times—not by invading enemies but by a series of earthquakes.

RUINS OF HISHAM'S PALACE
Hisham's Palace, in Jericho, was a royal hunting lodge. It was built in the 8th century A.D. but was never completed.

A FLOURISHING TOWN
The buildings in the Turkish town of Çatal Hüyük around 6000 B.C. included houses and workshops. Others seem to have been religious shrines. For safety, people lived in interconnecting, rectangular houses, with no doors. The rooftops acted as streets.

People used the rooftops as streets.

Wall paintings depicted vultures and headless men.

ÇATAL HÜYÜK, TURKEY

Built on a fertile river plain, the town of Çatal Hüyük was a successful farming settlement. Its wealth was also based on cattle-breeding and trade in obsidian (for making tools and weapons). By 6500 B.C., Çatal Hüyük was flourishing and some 5,000 people lived there.

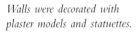

Walls were decorated with plaster models and statuettes.

Long wooden ladders to reach rooftops.

c. 9000 B.C. A shrine stands on the site of ancient Jericho in the Near East.

c. 8000 B.C. Jericho grows into a thriving town of some 2,000 people. It is one of the oldest known towns, built on the west bank of the river Jordan. The first bricks are made by Jericho's people.

c. 7000 B.C. Jericho is destroyed by an earthquake, but the town is later rebuilt. The Turkish town of Çatal Hüyük is founded. Its people are successful farmers and traders.

c. 6500 B.C. The oldest known textiles are made in Çatal Hüyük. They are linen, made from the fibers of the flax plant, and sewn into clothes.

MESOPOTAMIA AND SUMER

One of the world's earliest civilizations grew up on the fertile plains between the rivers Tigris and Euphrates. Now situated in Iraq, this area became known as Mesopotamia, "the land between the two rivers." In about 5000 B.C., a group of people called the Sumerians settled in the southern part of Mesopotamia. By about 3500 B.C., the original farming villages had grown into thriving towns and cities. Some of the larger settlements, such as Ur and Uruk, grew into cities, then into independent city-states. The cities were ruled by Councils of Elders.

The Sumerians were expert mathematicians and astronomers. They also devised a calendar and a legal system, and they adapted the potter's wheel for transportation.

Temple entrance

Their most important breakthrough, however, was the invention of a system of writing, known as cuneiform, in about 3500 B.C.

THE ZIGGURAT AT UR
This great ziggurat, or stepped temple, was built in Ur in about 2100 B.C. It was worshipped as the home of the Moon god, Nanna.

Platform

MAGNIFICENT JEWELS
This Sumerian woman's jewelry is made from gold and silver. The jewellery is inlaid with precious stones, such as lapis lazuli.

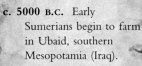

c. 5000 B.C. Early Sumerians begin to farm in Ubaid, southern Mesopotamia (Iraq).

c. 4000 B.C. The Sumerians learn how to smelt metal and use sailing boats on the Tigris and Euphrates rivers.

c. 3500 B.C. The Sumerians invent writing and the wheel. They discover how to make bronze from copper and tin.

c. 2900–2400 B.C. Kings are established in the main Sumerian cities.

c. 2400–2100 B.C. Sumer is conquered by the Akkadians, then by the Gutians.

c. 2100 B.C. The city of Ur reaches the height of its power under King Ur-Nammu.

c. 2000 B.C. Ur is destroyed by the Elamites. The Sumerian civilization comes to an end.

Main stairway

31

ANCIENT EGYPT

The first villages of ancient Egypt were established some 7,000 years ago. In time, these small settlements formed two kingdoms—Lower Egypt in the delta of the river Nile and Upper Egypt along the river valley. In about 3100 B.C., King Menes, the ruler of Upper Egypt, united the two kingdoms and built his capital at Memphis. He established the first dynasty (line of kings) of ancient Egypt.

Capstone

Limestone blocks

THE PYRAMIDS
The pyramids were built as tombs for the early pharaohs. They housed the pharaoh's body and priceless treasures to accompany him into the next world. The Great Pyramid of Giza was built for King Khufu some 4,600 years ago.

An outer coating of white casing blocks covered the whole pyramid.

QUEEN
NEFERTITI
*Nefertiti was the chief wife
of King Akhenaten, who
ruled Egypt from about
1364 B.C. to 1347 B.C.*

POWERFUL PHARAOHS

The king was the most powerful person in
ancient Egyptian society and every aspect of
Egyptian life was under his control. From
about 1554 B.C., the king was given the
honorary title of pharaoh. Two officials, called
viziers, helped him govern and collect taxes.
The country was divided into 42 districts, each
governed on the pharaoh's behalf by officials
called nomarchs. Further officials were put in
charge of the major state departments such as
the Treasury.

c. **5000–3100 B.C.** Nile
valley cultures appear.

c. **4000 B.C.** Boats on the
Nile begin to use sails.

c. **3200 B.C.** Early
hieroglyphs are used in
Egypt.

c. **3100 B.C.** King Menes
unites Lower and Upper
Egypt.

c. **3100–2686 B.C.** Archaic
Period.

c. **2686–2150 B.C.** The Old
Kingdom. The first
pyramids are built.

c. **2580 B.C.** The Sphinx
and Great Pyramid at
Giza are built.

c. **2150–2040 B.C.** First
Intermediate Period.

c. **2040–1640 B.C.** The
Middle Kingdom. King
Mentuhotep II reunites
Egypt and restores order.

c. **1640–1552 B.C.** The
Second Intermediate
Period (Dynasties 14 to
17). The Hyksos people
from Asia overrun
Egypt.

EGYPTIAN BELIEFS

The ancient Egyptians believed firmly in life after death. When a person died, their soul was thought to travel to an underworld, called Duat. Here the soul had to undergo a series of ordeals in order to progress to a better life in the next world.

For a person's soul to prosper in the next world, their body had to survive intact. The ancient Egyptians discovered how to preserve bodies by using the process of mummification. After the internal organs had been removed, the body was dried out, oiled, and wrapped in linen strips, then placed in its coffin. Animals were preserved in this way, too.

CANOPIC JARS
When a body was mummified, the dead person's internal organs (liver, lungs, stomach, and intestines) were removed. They were carefully wrapped and stored in four containers called canopic jars. The jars were placed in a chest inside the tomb.

Jar stopper

Hieroglyphs (picture writing)

*THE KINGDOM OF
THE GODS*
*The pharaoh's body was
taken to his tomb in a
decorated funeral barge. A
proper burial ensured a place
in Osiris' kingdom.*

Osiris Amun Isis Horus

THE VALLEY OF THE KINGS

The kings of the New Kingdom were buried
in tombs cut deep into a valley near Thebes,
called the Valley of the Kings. This was meant
to deter the tomb robbers who had stripped
the pyramid tombs bare.

Unfortunately, most of
these tombs were
ransacked too.

*The walls of tombs
were covered with paintings
of gods and goddesses.*

- **c. 1552–1085 B.C.** The
  New Kingdom in Egypt
  (Dynasties 18 to 20).

- **c. 1479–1425 B.C.** Reign
  of King Tuthmosis III.
  The Egyptian empire is
  at the height of its
  power.

- **c. 1347–1337 B.C.** Reign of
  King Tutankhamun.

- **c. 1085–664 B.C.** Third
  Intermediate Period
  (Dynasties 21 to 25).

- **c. 664–332 B.C.** The Late
  Period (Dynasties 26 to
  30).

- **c. 525–404 B.C.** The
  Persians invade Egypt
  and rule as Dynasty 27.

- **332 B.C.** Alexander the
  Great (founder of
  Alexandria) takes
  control of Egypt.

- **323 B.C.** Alexander dies.
  Egypt is ruled by the
  Ptolemies.

- **30 B.C.** Cleopatra, the last
  of the Ptolemies,
  commits suicide. Egypt
  becomes a province of
  the Roman empire.

THE INDUS VALLEY

Around 3000 B.C., another great early civilization grew up along the banks of the river Indus in ancient India (present-day Pakistan). Called the Indus Valley civilization, by 2500 B.C. it had reached the height of its power. Its two great centers were the cities of Harappa and Mohenjo Daro, each with a population of some 40,000 people. From about 2000 B.C., however, this mighty civilization began to decline. This may have been caused by flooding, by a change in the course of the Indus, or by overgrazing of the land.

Streets were laid out in a grid-like pattern.

The houses of mud brick had bathrooms and a drainage system.

The Great Bath

36

A TRADING CIVILIZATION

The Indus Valley civilization had a highly organized system of trade. Merchants traded grain and other agricultural produce, grown on the fertile river plains, as well as artifacts made by the cities' artists and craft workers. Goods were traded for precious metals and cloth.

MOHENJO DARO

Like other cities in the Indus valley, Mohenjo Daro was laid out on a grid pattern. Each city had a citadel, with important buildings, such as the Great Bath, used for religious rituals.

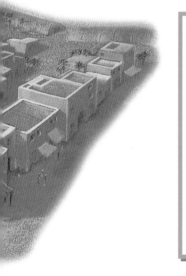

This map shows the extent and main cities of the Indus Valley civilization. This region now lies inside modern-day Pakistan.

c. 3000 B.C. Farming settlements grow up along the valley of the river Indus in northwest India (now Pakistan).

c. 2500 B.C. The Indus Valley civilization is at its height.

c. 2000 B.C. Some Indus sites start to show signs of decline.

c. 1500 B.C. The region is taken over by the Aryans, groups of Indo-Europeans from Iran. Their religious beliefs mix with those of the Indus cities to form the basis of the Hindu religion, which is still practiced in India today.

MEGALITHIC EUROPE

From about 4500 B.C., people in Europe began building monuments of massive, standing stones, called megaliths. These were placed in circles, or upright next to one another, with another stone laid horizontally on top.

Stone circles were laid out according to strict mathematical rules, but no one is sure what they were used for. They may have been observatories for studying the Sun, Moon, and stars, or temples for religious ceremonies. Experts also think that both human and animal sacrifices may have taken place inside the circles.

STONEHENGE, ENGLAND
The most famous stone circle is Stonehenge in England. Built from about 2800 B.C., the stones were positioned to align precisely with the rays of the Sun on June 21.

The largest stones form a horseshoe shape within the outer circle.

Outer circle of stones

MONUMENTS TO THE DEAD

Builders of megaliths constructed stone monuments over the graves of their dead. These were often long, passagelike chambers, lined with megaliths, and buried under a mound of earth, called a barrow. Offerings of food and drink were left at the entrance, for use in the next world.

Druid priest

DRUID WORSHIP
Druids used Stonehenge for their religious ceremonies centuries after it was built.

Fallen stone

c. **4500 B.C.** People start building megaliths in western Europe.

c. **4000 B.C.** First passage graves are built at Carnac, France.

c. **3200 B.C.** Newgrange grave is built in Ireland.

c. **2800–2000 B.C.** Stonehenge, England, is built. The monument was built in three stages.

c. **2750–2000 B.C.** Megalithic temples are built on the island of Malta.

THE MINOANS OF CRETE

The Minoan civilization was the first major civilization in Europe. It began on the island of Crete and was named after its ruler, King Minos. It was at the height of its power from about 2000 B.C. The Minoans had a rich and glittering culture, with a highly organized society and flourishing economy. Minoan merchants traveled throughout the Mediterranean, trading wine, grain, and olive oil, produced on the island, for luxury goods, such as amber, ivory, and precious metals.

THE PALACE OF KNOSSOS
Knossos was the largest Minoan palace. The walls of the royal apartments were decorated with frescos, or wall paintings, which have provided valuable clues about Minoan life.

Buildings were supported by short wooden columns.

MINOAN PALACES

Each large Minoan town was built around a splendid palace, housing hundreds or even thousands of people. Palaces were royal residences as well as trading centers. They also contained shrines, workshops, and living quarters for officials. By 1450 B.C., however, most of the palaces had been destroyed, probably by earthquakes or volcanic eruptions, and Crete was taken over by the Mycenaeans.

The central courtyard was used for religious ceremonies.

Knossos had a total of 1,300 rooms.

c. 6000 B.C. The first farmers settle in Crete.

c. 3000–1000 B.C. People on Crete and mainland Greece learn how to make bronze.

c. 2000 B.C. The first palaces are built on Crete.

c. 1700 B.C. The palaces are destroyed by earthquakes and are later rebuilt.

c. 1600 B.C. The first Mycenaeans reach Crete.

c. 1450 B.C. A volcanic eruption destroys all the palaces on Crete, including Knossos.

c. 1100 B.C. The end of the Minoan civilization.

THE MYCENAEANS

From about 1600 B.C. to 1100 B.C. the Mycenaeans dominated mainland Greece. They lived in separate, small kingdoms, although they shared the same language and beliefs and are named after their greatest city, Mycenae. Here evidence of their culture was first discovered. The Mycenaeans built their great palaces on hill tops, surrounded by massive stone walls. This type of fortified city was called an acropolis, which means "high city" in Greek. These fortifications made their cities much easier to defend from attack.

MYSTERY OF THE MASK
This gold death mask was believed by Heinrich Schliemann to cover the face of Agamemnon, the legendary king of Mycenae. Modern scholars, however, think that the graves found by Schliemann date from about 300 years before Agamemnon's time.

THE TROJAN HORSE
According to legend, the Trojan War began when Mycenaean soldiers were smuggled into the city of Troy inside a huge wooden horse.

GOLDEN TREASURE

In 1876, the German archaeologist Heinrich Schliemann began excavating a circle of stone slabs inside the city walls of Mycenae. He discovered five graves, sunk deep into the ground. They contained the bodies of 16 members of the Mycenaean royal family, five of whom had gold death masks covering their faces. Alongside lay a priceless hoard of golden treasure.

GATEWAY TO MYCENAE
The Lion Gate, the main gateway into Mycenae, was built in about 1250 B.C. The two carved lions may have been symbols of the Mycenaean royal family.

c. 1600–1100 B.C. The Mycenaeans dominate mainland Greece.

c. 1450 B.C. The Mycenaeans become rulers of Crete.

c. 1250 B.C. The traditional date of the fall of Troy.

c. 1200 B.C. Mycenaean culture begins to decline, possibly due to crop failure and a weak economy. People begin to abandon the great cities.

c. 1100–800 B.C. The Dark Ages in Greece.

ANCIENT CHINA

The earliest civilizations in China grew up along the banks of three major rivers—the Chang Jiang (Yangtze), Xi Jiang (West River), and Huang He (Yellow River). From about 2205 B.C., China was ruled by a series of dynasties (families). The Shang Dynasty ruled for more than 400 years before being conquered by the Zhou Dynasty. During the reign of the Zhou, many wars were fought between rival kingdoms, but it was also a period of economic growth and of trading success, with Chinese silk, precious jade, and fine porcelain being traded abroad.

THE GREAT WALL OF CHINA
The Great Wall, built between 214 and 204 B.C., formed a huge barrier high and wide enough for chariots to drive along it.

A military overseer

A worker uses a yoke to carry a heavy load.

Convicted criminals helped to build the wall.

CONFUCIUS
The prophet and philosopher
Confucius dedicated himself to
teaching people how to live in
peace. His thoughts and
teachings influenced many
Chinese people.

THE QIN DYNASTY

Gradually, the warlike
Qin (or Ch'in) Dynasty
united the country and
established the empire
that gives China its
name. The first
emperor, Shi Huangdi,
reorganized government
and standardized money, weights, and
measures. The Qin built the Great Wall of
China to keep out the hostile Hsung Nu
people (the Huns), as well as an extensive road
and canal network.

Watch tower

Nobles watched the building work.

Pulley to lift earth from works below.

Bamboo scaffold

c. 1766–1027 B.C. The
Shang dynasty rules
China.

1027–256 B.C. The Zhou
dynasty rules China.

c. 551 B.C. Birth of the
great teacher, Confucius.

481–221 B.C. The so-called
Warring States Period
when most of China is
in civil war.

221 B.C. Shi Huangdi
unites China and founds
the Qin dynasty. He
becomes China's first
emperor.

212 B.C. Shi Huangdi burns
books that contain
different ideas from his
own.

210 B.C. Death of Shi
Huangdi. He was buried
with a vast army of
10,000 life-sized clay
soldiers.

202 B.C. Qin dynasty
collapses and the Han
dynasty rules China
until A.D. 9.

45

EARLY WRITING

About 5,500 years ago the Sumerians invented the first fully developed system of writing, called cuneiform. It represented words with symbols made up of wedge-shaped strokes. (The name cuneiform means "wedge-shaped.") These were impressed onto wet clay, using a reed pen, and the clay tablets were baked hard in the sun. The Sumerians used cuneiform to keep temple records and merchants' accounts. At about the same time, the ancient Egyptians were using a system of picture writing known as hieroglyphics. Each picture, or hieroglyph, stood for a picture or sound. Hieroglyphs were extremely complicated so highly trained scribes were employed to read and write them.

Cuneiform tablet

Hindu symbol "Om" (the name of God).

PICTURE SYMBOLS

In the earliest writing systems, picture symbols were used to represent either words or individual characters. In some systems, such as the Chinese one, several thousand characters were in use. At first, these characters were drawn as picture symbols but they gradually became more abstract in form.

Arab numerals

COMMUNICATION THROUGH PICTURES

This cave painting was made thousands of years before any proper system of writing was developed.

LETTERS AND NUMBERS

By about 1000 B.C., the Phoenicians used a simple alphabet of 22 letters. A Greek version was adapted by the Romans for writing Latin (the basis of today's English alphabet). Numerals (1, 2, 3 etc.) were developed from a number system used by Hindus in India.

Phoenician alphabet

Hieroglyphic tablet

Chinese writing

米	𝕯	𢑚	*around 1500 B.C.*
朩	𝒟	𨐔	*before 213 B.C.*
木	月	鳥	*after A.D. 200*

tree   moon   bird

- **c. 3500 B.C.** The Sumerians invent the cuneiform writing system.
- **c. 3500 B.C.** Hieroglyphs are used for the first time in Egypt.
- **c. 2500 B.C.** Merchants from the Indus Valley civilization use carved stone seals bearing a written inscription, possibly the merchant's name.
- **c. 1766–1027 B.C.** During the reign of China's Shang dynasty people predict the future using oracle bones decorated with early Chinese writing.
- **1027–256 B.C.** During the Zhou dynasty Chinese writing consists of several thousand characters.
- **c. 1000 B.C.** The Phoenician alphabet is well developed.
- **c. 727 B.C.** The Greeks adopt the Phoenician alphabet.

PHOENICIANS

The greatest traders and seafarers of the ancient world were the Phoenicians. They lived along the eastern coast of the Mediterranean (now part of Syria, Lebanon, and Israel). Here, in about 1500 B.C., they founded their greatest cities—Tyre, their main port, and Sidon. These became the flourishing centers of a vast trading network. The Phoenicians traded goods, such as glassware, timber, cedar oil, purple-dyed cloth, and ivory throughout the Mediterranean, venturing as far west as Britain and down the African coast. In return they bought silver, copper, and tin.

GREAT SEAFARERS

The Phoenicians had magnificent ships made of cedar wood—long, fast galleys for war and broader, sturdier ships for trade. They were also expert navigators, relying on the winds and stars to find their way.

TRADE ROUTES
This map shows the main trade routes and trading colonies of the Phoenicians.

Colonized areas
Marseille
SPAIN
Gadir (Cadiz)
SARDINIA
SICILY
Black Sea
Tingis (Tangier)
Carthage
MALTA
CRETE
PHOENICIA
CYPRUS
Byblos
Sidon
Colonized areas
Mediterranean Sea
Tyre
AFRICA
Ugarit (Ras Shamra)

Rows of oarsmen

Look-out post

The large square
sail harnessed
the power of the
wind.

The cargo was
tightly lashed to
the deck.

A Phoenician trading ship used
both sails and oars to give it greater
maneuverability and speed. The
oarsmen allowed the ship to sail in any
direction. A lookout kept watch for pirates who might
attempt to steal the valuable cargo.

c. 1200 B.C. The beginning
of the Phoenicians' rise
to power.

c. 1200–350 B.C. The
Phoenicians are the
leading trading nation in
the Mediterranean.

c. 1140 B.C. The
Phoenician colony of
Utica is founded in
North Africa.

c. 1000 B.C. The
Phoenician alphabet is
well developed.

c. 814 B.C. The city of
Carthage is founded in
North Africa.

729 B.C. The Assyrian king,
Shalmaneser V, invades
Phoenicia.

c. 727 B.C. The Greeks
adopt the Phoenician
alphabet.

332 B.C. Alexander the
Great conquers
Phoenicia.

146 B.C. Rome defeats the
Phoenician colony of
Carthage at the end of
the Punic Wars.

ANCIENT AMERICA

From about 1200 B.C., two great civilizations grew up in ancient America—the Olmecs in western Mexico and the Chavin along the coast of northern Peru. Their ancestors had crossed the Bering Strait from Asia to America thousands of years before. The Olmec civilization began in about 1500 B.C. around the Gulf of Mexico. One of the main centers of Olmec culture was La Venta, whose people earned their living by fishing the rich waters and farming. The Olmecs were also skilled artists and craft workers, producing hundreds of sculptures and carvings from stone, jade, and clay.

OLMEC CARVINGS
These tiny jade and serpentine figures were found at La Venta in 1955. They had been carefully buried with sand.

PYRAMID BUILDERS
The Olmecs built huge stepped pyramids made of earth. Here they worshiped their gods and performed religious ceremonies. The pyramid at La Venta was 111 feet (34 m) high. Around it lay several squares that were paved to look like jaguar masks.

THE CHAVIN CIVILIZATION

The Chavin civilization, which is named after the town Chavin de Huantar in the Andes, began in Peru in about 1200 B.C. and lasted for about 1,000 years. Chavin de Huantar was a religious center, with a huge temple surrounded by a maze of rooms and passageways.

c. 1200–300 B.C. The Olmec civilization flourishes on the coast of western Mexico.

c. 1200–200 B.C. The Chavin civilization flourishes on the coast of northern Peru.

c. 1100 B.C. Olmecs build a great ceremonial center at San Lorenzo.

c. 1000 B.C. Olmec city of La Venta becomes a major center for fishing, farming, and trade.

c. 850–200 B.C. Chavin de Huantar in the Peruvian Andes is at the height of its power.

c. 700 B.C. Olmecs abandon San Lorenzo.

c. 400–300 B.C. La Venta is abandoned and destroyed.

ASSYRIANS

In about 2000 B.C., the Assyrians gained their independence from their powerful neighbors in Sumer and Akkad. They established a line of warrior-kings, under whose leadership they conquered a mighty empire, which was at its greatest during the New Assyrian empire (around 1000–612 B.C.). The Assyrians were tough, fearless soldiers. They ruled by force and showed no mercy.

Shield

Iron-tipped battering ram

Archer

52

HITTITE WARRIORS
The Hittites were a warlike people from Anatolia (in modern-day Turkey). They were the first to use chariots for warfare.

"KINGS OF THE UNIVERSE"

The Assyrian kings believed that they had been chosen to rule by the gods and so represented the gods on Earth. They were given grand titles such as the "King of the Universe." The king was head of the government and army, and he was also responsible for the temples and priests. To display their wealth and power, kings built magnificent cities and palaces. Palace walls were decorated with carved reliefs of conquests as well as showing scenes from everyday life.

Assault tower

UNDER ATTACK
The Assyrian army used fearsome assault towers mounted on wheels to breach (break through) the city walls of their enemies. The towers had iron-tipped battering rams that could be swung to either side to smash through walls and doors.

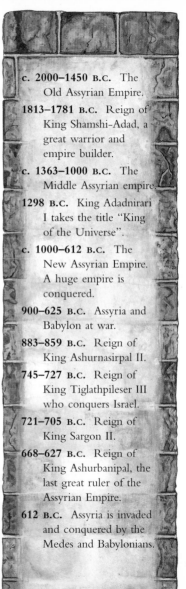

c. 2000–1450 B.C. The Old Assyrian Empire.

1813–1781 B.C. Reign of King Shamshi-Adad, a great warrior and empire builder.

c. 1363–1000 B.C. The Middle Assyrian empire.

1298 B.C. King Adadnirari I takes the title "King of the Universe".

c. 1000–612 B.C. The New Assyrian Empire. A huge empire is conquered.

900–625 B.C. Assyria and Babylon at war.

883–859 B.C. Reign of King Ashurnasirpal II.

745–727 B.C. Reign of King Tiglathpileser III who conquers Israel.

721–705 B.C. Reign of King Sargon II.

668–627 B.C. Reign of King Ashurbanipal, the last great ruler of the Assyrian Empire.

612 B.C. Assyria is invaded and conquered by the Medes and Babylonians.

53

BABYLONIANS

Babylon first grew powerful under the rule of King Hammurabi (c. 1792–1750 B.C.). He conquered the other kingdoms in Mesopotamia and extended Babylon's frontiers, making the city of Babylon capital of his new empire. Hammurabi's code of civil and criminal law is the oldest surviving legal code in the world. After his death, Babylon declined in power and was invaded by the Hittites, Kassites, Chaldeans and Assyrians. In the sixth century B.C., King Nebuchadnezzar II conquered a huge empire and Babylon regained its former glory. The Persians captured the kingdom in 539 B.C.

The gardens were planted with exotic flowers and trees.

Upper terrace

THE HANGING GARDENS OF BABYLON

One of the Seven Wonders of the ancient world, the Hanging Gardens were built during the reign of Nebuchadnezzar II. According to legend, his Persian wife missed the green hills of her homeland and so created her own terraced gardens.

THE CITY OF BABYLON

Situated on the banks of the river Euphrates (in modern Iraq), Babylon was a major trading center. It was also a flourishing religious complex, especially for the worship of the god Marduk, patron of the city. Nebuchadnezzar II rebuilt Babylon in magnificent style.

Water was taken from the Euphrates to water the gardens.

Lower terrace

THE GRANDEST GATE
One of eight massive city gates, the Ishtar Gate marked Babylon's northern entrance. It was named for the goddess of love and war.

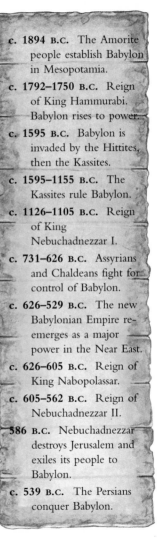

c. 1894 B.C. The Amorite people establish Babylon in Mesopotamia.

c. 1792–1750 B.C. Reign of King Hammurabi. Babylon rises to power.

c. 1595 B.C. Babylon is invaded by the Hittites, then the Kassites.

c. 1595–1155 B.C. The Kassites rule Babylon.

c. 1126–1105 B.C. Reign of King Nebuchadnezzar I.

c. 731–626 B.C. Assyrians and Chaldeans fight for control of Babylon.

c. 626–529 B.C. The new Babylonian Empire re-emerges as a major power in the Near East.

c. 626–605 B.C. Reign of King Nabopolassar.

c. 605–562 B.C. Reign of Nebuchadnezzar II.

586 B.C. Nebuchadnezzar destroys Jerusalem and exiles its people to Babylon.

c. 539 B.C. The Persians conquer Babylon.

55

ANCIENT GREECE

By about 800 B.C., Greece saw the rise of a new civilization whose influence has lasted to the present day. Ancient Greece was divided into independent city-states, the two most important being Athens and Sparta. Most city-states were ruled by wealthy nobles and later, following revolts, by absolute rulers called tyrants. In about 508 B.C., a new type of government called democracy was introduced in Athens. It gave every male citizen a say in the running of the city. When the Persians invaded Greece in 490 B.C., the city-states joined forces and defeated the invaders.

Bronze helmet

A heavy round shield protected the soldier's body.

Split skirtlike tunic

IN BATTLE

A hoplite, or foot soldier, was the most important part of the Greek army. Greek hoplites formed a phalanx—a block of soldiers eight or more rows deep.

Leg armor

BATTLE SHIPS
Greek warships had sails and several banks of oars on either side, which made them very fast and easy to maneuver.

DEFEAT BY SPARTA

Greece's newly won security did not last long and, in 431 B.C., war broke out between Athens and Sparta. The Peloponnesian Wars lasted for 27 years and tore the country apart. The Spartans besieged Athens and the city finally surrendered in 404 B.C.

- **c. 900 B.C.** State of Sparta founded by the Dorians.
- **c. 800–500 B.C.** The Archaic Period. Greece revives after The Dark Ages, a period of decline.
- **776 B.C.** The first Olympic Games are held.
- **c. 500–336 B.C.** Greek culture reaches its height in the Classical Period.
- **490–449 B.C.** The Persian Wars. Greece wins.
- **479–431 B.C.** Athens prospers.
- **447–438 B.C.** The Parthenon is built in Athens.
- **431–404 B.C.** The Peloponnesian Wars between Athens and Sparta. Sparta wins.
- **371 B.C.** Sparta is defeated by Thebes.
- **338 B.C.** The Macedonians defeat the Greeks.
- **336–30 B.C.** The Hellenistic Period.
- **147–146 B.C.** Greece becomes part of the Roman Empire.

GREEK CULTURE

Greek civilization came to an end more than 2,000 years ago, yet its influence on politics, philosophy, art and architecture, language, and literature can still be felt today. Much of our language and many of our ideas about science and art come from the ancient Greeks, who were great scholars, thinkers, and teachers. At first, they answered questions about life and nature with stories about the gods. Later, they started to look for more practical, more scientific ways of understanding the world about them.

Circular area for acting.

The actors (all male) wore masks.

The audience sat on stone seats arranged in rows.

THE OLYMPIC GAMES

Sport in ancient Greece was not only a means of entertainment, but also a way of keeping men fit and healthy for fighting. The oldest and most famous competition for athletes was the Olympic Games, held every four years at Olympia, in honor of Zeus. Athletes trained hard for many months before the games.

EVERYDAY LIFE
Much of our knowledge about the ancient Greeks comes from vases and vessels. They were decorated with scenes from daily life showing what the Greeks wore, how they lived and so on.

GREEK THEATER
Drama played a very important part in the lives of the ancient Greeks. At first, plays were performed in the market place. Later, open-air theaters like this one were built across Greece. The largest could hold an audience of 18,000 people.

PERICLES, the most famous politician of Athens' Golden Age, ordered the building of the Parthenon.

SOCRATES was one of the most influential Greek philosophers.

ZEUS, the king of gods, was head of the Olympians, a family of gods and goddesses from Mount Olympus.

DARIUS I led his troops against Greece during the Persian Wars. They were defeated in 480 B.C.

ALEXANDER THE GREAT

While the city-states of Greece were in disarray following the Peloponnesian Wars, the new power of Macedonia took full advantage of the situation. When Philip II came to the throne in 359 B.C., he transformed Macedonia into the greatest military force of the day. In 338 B.C., at the battle of Chaeronea, Philip's army gained control of Greece, uniting the Greeks and Macedonians against the Persians. In 336 B.C. Philip was assassinated and the throne passed to his son, Alexander. Under Alexander's leadership, the Macedonian empire became the largest in the ancient world.

A GREAT LEADER
Alexander was an even more brilliant leader and general than his father, Philip II. This is Alexander on his favorite horse, Bucephalus..

ALEXANDER'S EMPIRE
The map shows the extent of Alexander's empire and the routes of his campaigns. It took Alexander just 13 years to conquer a vast empire stretching from Greece eastward to India.

MACEDONIA

BLACK SEA

Granicus · ASIA MINOR

GREECE

MEDITERRANEAN SEA

· Issus

Tyre ·

Alexandria

EGYPT

RED SEA

CONQUERING THE PERSIANS

Alexander conquered the Persians not only to acquire their lands but also to replenish his treasuries with their wealth. By 331 B.C. he was king of the whole of Persia. To strengthen ties with the Persians, Alexander wore Persian clothes and married a Persian princess.

CASPIAN SEA

Gaugamela

PARTHIA

Babylon
Susa

PERSIA

BACTRIA

Persepolis

PERSIAN
GULF

GEDROSIA

→ Route of Alexander's campaigns

Maximum extent of the empir

359 B.C. Philip II becomes King of Macedonia.

356 B.C. Alexander is born.

338 B.C. At Chaeronea, Philip wins control of the Greek city-states.

336 B.C. Philip is murdered. Alexander becomes king at the age of 20.

333 B.C. Alexander defeats the Persians at the battle of Issus.

332 B.C. Alexander marches on and conquers Egypt.

331 B.C. Alexander defeats the Persians at the battle of Gaugamela. Darius is assassinated and Alexander becomes King of Persia.

324 B.C. Alexander's tired army mutinies in India.

323 B.C. Alexander dies of a fever in Babylon.

323–281 B.C. The empire is split into three—Persia, Egypt, and Macedonia.

147–146 B.C. Macedonia becomes part of the Roman Empire.

THE CELTS

The Celts probably first lived in France and Austria from about 600 B.C. Gradually, Celtic tribes spread across southern and western Europe, conquering the lands and settling in hill-forts and farms. Famed and feared for their bravery in battle, the Celts were great warriors and individual warriors often fought on their own. Wars frequently broke out between the rival Celtic tribes. This helped the Romans to defeat the Celts more easily than if they had been a unified and efficiently run military force. Following defeat, much of their territory was brought under Roman rule.

Timber framework

Animals kept in fenced area beside hut.

LIFE IN A HILL-FORT
Safe within a hill-fort, each family lived with their animals in circular wooden huts with thatched roofs. The hill-forts were built on high ground to give a clear view of the surrounding countryside and of any intruders.

CELTIC CULTURE

The Celts were highly skilled metalsmiths, making beautifully decorated weapons and jewelry. They were gifted poets and musicians, passing down stories and history by word of mouth. The Celts worshipped many gods and goddesses, offering sacrifices in their honor. Religious ceremonies were performed by priests, called druids.

A huge iron cooking cauldron hung over the fire in the center of the hut.

Cloth made of woven wool.

QUEEN BOUDICCA
In A.D. 60, Boudicca (or Boadicea), the queen of the Iceni tribe from East Anglia, led a revolt against the Romans in Britain.

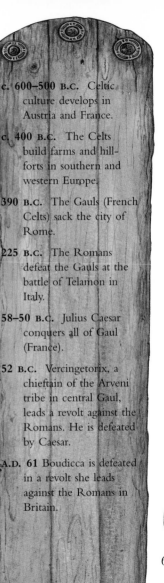

c. 600–500 B.C. Celtic culture develops in Austria and France.

c. 400 B.C. The Celts build farms and hill-forts in southern and western Europe.

390 B.C. The Gauls (French Celts) sack the city of Rome.

225 B.C. The Romans defeat the Gauls at the battle of Telamon in Italy.

58–50 B.C. Julius Caesar conquers all of Gaul (France).

52 B.C. Vercingetorix, a chieftain of the Arveni tribe in central Gaul, leads a revolt against the Romans. He is defeated by Caesar.

A.D. 61 Boudicca is defeated in a revolt she leads against the Romans in Britain.

63

THE ROMANS

Spear

From its humble beginnings as a small group of villages populated by criminals and slaves, Rome grew to become the capital of the most powerful empire the western world had ever seen. At first, Rome was ruled by kings, until about 509 B.C. when King Tarquin the Proud was expelled. For the next 500 years Rome was a republic. Power passed to the Senate, a law-making body made up of important nobles. It was headed by two elected officials, called consuls, who managed the affairs of the Senate and the Roman army.

THE ROMAN ARMY

Small units of Roman soldiers, called centuries, consisted of 100 men and were commanded by centurions. A soldier carried two basic weapons—a spear to throw as he neared the enemy, and a short sword for close combat.

Long shield

AN EMPIRE IS BORN

By about 50 B.C., Rome had conquered most of the lands around the Mediterranean. However, rivalry between army generals and tensions between rich and poor plunged Rome into civil war. The republic crumbled, and in 27 B.C. Octavian, son of Julius Caesar, became the first Roman emperor.

ROMULUS AND REMUS

According to legend, Rome was founded by twin brothers called Romulus and Remus. They were rescued by a she-wolf after being abandoned.

753 B.C. The founding of Rome.

c. 509 B.C. The founding of the Roman Republic.

49 B.C. Julius Caesar is dictator of Rome.

27 B.C. The end of the Republic. Octavian is the first emperor.

A.D. 64 Fire devastates Rome.

c. A.D. 80 The Colosseum is completed in Rome.

A.D. 98–117 The empire is at its greatest extent.

A.D. 117–138 Hadrian rules.

A.D. 166–167 The empire is devastated by a plague.

A.D. 286 Diocletian divides the empire into west and east.

A.D. 391 Christianity becomes the official religion of the Roman Empire.

A.D. 410 Alaric the Goth sacks Rome.

A.D. 476 The last western emperor, Romulus Augustulus, is deposed.

65

ROMAN SOCIETY

The amazing expansion and success of the Roman empire was due largely to its army, the best trained and best equipped in the world. Soldiers were paid wages and joined up for 20 to 25 years. For many young men from good families, the army provided a stepping stone to a glittering political career. Ordinary soldiers were grouped into units, called legions, each made up of about 5,000 men. The legions, in turn, were made up of smaller units, called centuries, of 100 men commanded by soldiers called centurions.

Augustus was the first emperor of Rome.

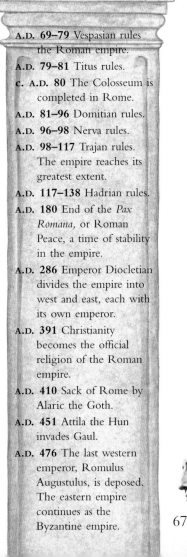

In 218 B.C., during the Punic Wars, the Carthaginian general, Hannibal, led a surprise attack on the Romans by marching over the Alps with 35,000 men and 37 elephants.

Roman society was divided into citizens and non citizens. There were three classes of citizens—patricians, the richest and most influential aristocrats; equites, the wealthy merchants, and plebians, the ordinary citizens, or "commoners." All citizens were allowed to vote in elections and to serve in the army. They were also allowed to wear togas. Noncitizens included provincials, people who lived outside Rome itself but in territory under Roman rule, and slaves. Slaves had no rights or status. They were owned by wealthy citizens, or by the government, and did all the hardest, dirtiest jobs.

A.D. 69–79 Vespasian rules the Roman empire.

A.D. 79–81 Titus rules.

c. A.D. 80 The Colosseum is completed in Rome.

A.D. 81–96 Domitian rules.

A.D. 96–98 Nerva rules.

A.D. 98–117 Trajan rules. The empire reaches its greatest extent.

A.D. 117–138 Hadrian rules.

A.D. 180 End of the *Pax Romana,* or Roman Peace, a time of stability in the empire.

A.D. 286 Emperor Diocletian divides the empire into west and east, each with its own emperor.

A.D. 391 Christianity becomes the official religion of the Roman empire.

A.D. 410 Sack of Rome by Alaric the Goth.

A.D. 451 Attila the Hun invades Gaul.

A.D. 476 The last western emperor, Romulus Augustulus, is deposed. The eastern empire continues as the Byzantine empire.

EMPIRES OF AFRICA

 The first great African civilization, apart from ancient Egypt, grew up in Nubia (now in northern Sudan) around 2000 B.C. It was the kingdom of Kush. In the third century B.C., the capital of Kush moved to Meroe, on the river Nile. The city became an important center of iron-working. In western Africa (now in Nigeria), another iron-working center developed in about 600 B.C. These people, known as the Nok, mined iron and used it to make farming tools, arrowheads, and spears.

A NOK VILLAGE
Life in a Nok village centered on farming and iron-working. The Nok smelted iron ore in a cylindrical pit furnace made of clay. This separated the metal from the rock. Potters used furnaces to fire their clay sculptures.

Goats provided milk and meat.

The people of Axum built stone obelisks. These huge towers may have been symbols of power or burial monuments for royalty.

THE KINGDOM OF AXUM

In northeast Africa (now in Ethiopia), the kingdom of Axum grew rich from buying and selling spices, incense, and ivory. Its major trading partners were Arabia, Egypt, and Persia. Although the people of Axum originally worshiped local gods, by the end of the fifth century A.D. most had become Christians.

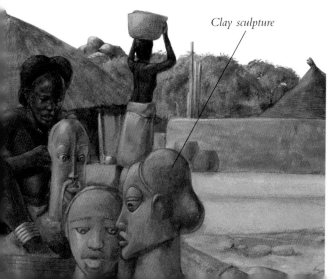

Clay sculpture

From 2000 B.C. The kingdom of Kush begins in Nubia.

c. 900 B.C. Kush gains its independence from Egypt.

c. 600 B.C. The Nok culture begins in northern Nigeria.

c. A.D. 200 The Nok culture ends but has a lasting effect on the artistic styles of Africa.

2nd century A.D. The kingdom of Axum rises to power.

A.D. 320–350 King Ezana rules Axum and converts to Christianity.

c. A.D. 350 Axum overruns the city of Meroe and brings the Kushite kingdom to an end.

6th century A.D. Axum rules part of western Arabia.

c. A.D. 1000 The kingdom of Axum collapses as a new Islamic empire from Arabia expands.

69

EMPIRES OF INDIA

In about 321 B.C., a young prince, Chandragupta Maurya, founded the first Indian empire stretching across northern India. Chandragupta's grandson, Ashoka, who came to the throne in 269 B.C., extended the empire farther, until most of India came under Mauryan rule. Following a bloody battle against the people of Kalinga in eastern India, Ashoka was sickened by the killing and bloodshed. Filled with remorse, he converted to Buddhism and vowed from then on to follow its teachings of peace and nonviolence. Ashoka traveled throughout his empire, listening to people's views and complaints.

The gateway to the great stupa of Sanchi, part of which is shown here, was built during Ashok's reign. Stupas are dome-shaped Buddhist shrines.

THE GUPTA EMPIRE

After the Mauryan empire collapsed, India was divided into several smaller states and kingdoms. The Guptas from the Ganges valley extended their power, ruling northern India for 200 years. Under Chandra Gupta II, India enjoyed a Golden Age. The arts flourished, and Hinduism became the main religion.

EMPEROR ASHOKA MAURYA
Ashoka, one of India's greatest rulers, has had a lasting effect on modern India. Its national emblem is copied from a pillar that Ashoka built, topped with four lions and four wheels.

- **c. 563 B.C.** Buddha is born in Lumbini, Nepal.
- **c. 483 B.C.** Buddha dies in Kushinagara, India.
- **c. 321 B.C.** Chandragupta seizes power and founds the Mauryan dynasty.
- **269–232 B.C.** Reign of Ashoka Maurya.
- **260 B.C.** Ashoka converts to Buddhism after the battle of Kalinga.
- **c. 185 B.C.** The Shunga Dynasty replaces the Mauryans.
- **c. A.D. 320** The beginnings of Gupta power emerges in the Ganges valley.
- **c. A.D. 350–550** The Gupta empire brings a Golden Age of Hinduism to India.
- **A.D. 380–415** The reign of Chandra Gupta II.
- **c. A.D. 550** Hun invasions weaken Gupta power. The empire splits into smaller kingdoms.

71

THE MIDDLE AGES

Kings and conflicts 500–1400

The period from about 500 to 1400 in Europe is known as the Middle Ages, or the medieval period. It began with the fall of the Roman empire and ended with the Renaissance, when a revival of art and learning swept through Europe. The medieval period was an age of wars and conquests. Some wars were fought to gain more

territory while others were wars of religion, fought between people of differing faiths in an age when religion dominated most people's lives. At this time China's civilization was further advanced than the rest of the world. Africa and the Americas saw the emergence of strong, well-organized empires based on trade, while the spread of Islam from Arabia across the Middle East and into North Africa and Spain brought a new way of life to a vast area. But most ordinary people lived simply, as farmers in villages or as craftworkers in towns.

BYZANTIUM

Following the collapse of the western half of the Roman Empire in 476, Roman rule in the east continued to flourish under what is called the Byzantine Empire. The Greek city-port of Byzantium (modern Istanbul in Turkey) was the capital of this eastern empire, and the center of the eastern Christian Church. Under Emperor Justinian, the Byzantine Empire reached its peak in the 500s. Justinian issued a code of laws on which the legal system in many European countries was later based.

AT THE RACES

Chariot races were more than just thrilling entertainment. Watched by the emperor, howling mobs in the Hippodrome cheered for one or other of the rival political factions in Byzantium.

CONSTANTINE THE GREAT
Constantine, the first Christian emperor of
Rome, moved the empire's capital to
Byzantium and renamed it Constantinople.

BYZANTINE LIFE

Most of the empire's people were farmers,
living in small villages. Traders came to sell
goods in the towns, and Constantinople was a
bustling port and meeting place. The
Byzantines appreciated music, poetry, and art.
They decorated their churches, such as Hagia
Sophia in Constantinople, with fine frescoes
(wall paintings) and mosaics.

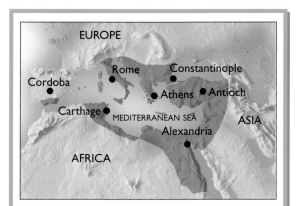

A GREAT EMPIRE
This map shows the Byzantine Empire at its height, in
the 500s. It included Italy, Greece, and Turkey as well
as parts of Spain and North Africa.

c. 306–337 Reign of
Constantine the Great.

330 Constantinople is
founded.

476 Fall of the western half
of the Roman Empire.

c. 501 A long series of wars
with Persia begins.

527–565 Reign of Justinian I.

678 An Arab siege of
Constantinople is
defeated.

900s Second golden age.
The Balkans and Russia
come under Byzantine
influence.

1054 Christian Church in
Constantinople breaks
with church in Rome.

1081 Alexius I Comnenus
seizes power and
introduces reforms.

1200 Empire begins to break
up under attacks from
Turks and Bulgarians.

1204 Constantinople is
sacked by Crusaders.

1341–1354 Civil war in the
empire.

1453 The Turks capture
Constantinople—end of
the Byzantine Empire.

75

THE FRANKS

The Franks were the strongest of the western European peoples who struggled for power after the collapse of the Roman Empire. By 540, under their leader Clovis, they had conquered most of the old Roman province of Gaul (modern France, which is named after the Franks). Clovis brought all the Frankish tribes under his control, and governed his lands through Church bishops and noblemen. In order to defend their estates and to conquer new lands, Frankish nobles and lords needed servants for military service. In return for this service, the servants were granted land.

FRANKISH METALWORK
These gold and enamel buckles would have been worn by a Frankish noble or warrior chief.

Plows were fitted with wheels

A team of oxen pulled the plow

The Franks tilled their fields in strips.

RIDING TO BATTLE
Frankish warriors, with their shaven heads and topknots, were formidable cavalry fighters. They wore light mail armor and used a curved throwing ax and a two-handed broadsword.

THE FRANKS FIGHT ON

In 687, a new ruling family was founded by Pepin of Herstal, chief of the Austrasian clan. The Franks went on fighting. Under Pepin, and later under his son, Charles Martel, Frankish territory expanded. Martel defeated Muslim invaders in 732.

FARMING THE LAND
The Franks were farmers. Frankish peasants plowed the fields on estates, called manors, which belonged to nobles or lords. With the help of wheeled plows, the Franks were able to farm land that had not been previously farmed.

350 Franks brought under Roman rule.

428 Franks from the Netherlands and lower Rhineland invade Gaul, led by King Chlodio.

451 Franks join with Romans to defeat Attila the Hun.

481–511 Reign of Clovis, founder of the Merovingian Dynasty.

486 Franks defeat the last great Roman army in the West, at Soissons.

506 Franks defeat the Visigoths.

540 Franks control most of Gaul and also lands in what is now Germany.

600 Rival Frankish clans, the Austrasians and the Neustrians, fight for power.

687 Austrasian chief, Pepin of Herstal, becomes the most powerful Frankish leader.

732 Charles Martel, Pepin's son, defeats the Muslim army at the battle of Poitiers.

751 End of the Merovingian Dynasty.

THE RISE OF ISLAM

In about 610, an Arab merchant named Muhammad preached a new religion, Islam (meaning "submission to the will of God"). His teachings were written down in the Koran, the holy book of Islam. In 622 Muhammad was driven out of his home town of Mecca by opponents who resented his teachings. His journey from Mecca to Yathrib (now Medina) is known as the Hegira, and marks the start of the Islamic calendar. The religion Muhammad preached changed the course of history, creating a new Muslim state that would defeat much larger empires.

BEHIND PALACE DOORS
A European view of life in the palace of a Muslim ruler. Islamic law permitted a man to have four wives.

MUHAMMAD
FLEES MECCA
After fleeing Mecca
Muhammad went into
hiding, with only a spider
for company.

A MUSLIM ASTRONOMER

Muslim astronomers observed the stars. They followed the ideas of the Greek astronomer Ptolemy about the universe.

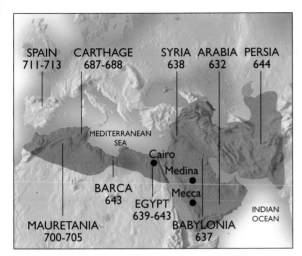

SPAIN 711-713

CARTHAGE 687-688

SYRIA 638

ARABIA 632

PERSIA 644

MEDITERRANEAN SEA

BARCA 643

Cairo

Medina

Mecca

EGYPT 639-643

MAURETANIA 700-705

BABYLONIA 637

INDIAN OCEAN

THE SPREAD OF ISLAM
Islamic conquests beyond Arabia began in 634. Over 81 years Islam spread from Persia in the east to Spain in the west.

A GROWING EMPIRE

After Muhammad's death, his followers spread Islam by preaching and by conquest. By 661 the Ummayad family controlled the growing Islamic Empire from their capital, Damascus. Muslims controlled most of the Middle East and North Africa. In 750 the Abbasid rulers moved the empire's capital to Baghdad.

610 Muhammad begins preaching in Mecca.

622 Flight to Yathrib (Medina), known as the Hegira.

630 Muhammad's army captures Mecca.

632 Muhammad dies. Islam begins to spread beyond Arabia.

634 Abu Bakr, the first caliph (successor), completes conquest of Arabia.

638 Syria and Jerusalem are conquered.

644 Caliph Omar is murdered and is succeeded by Othman.

661 The Islamic capital moves from Mecca to Damascus.

698 Arabs capture Carthage in North Africa.

750 Abbasid Dynasty is founded.

762 Abbasids make Baghdad capital of the empire.

786 Caliph Harun al-Rashid brings unity to the Islamic Empire.

MAYAN CIVILIZATIONS

Many impressive civilizations flourished in North and South America. The people of these civilizations built clifftop palaces, huge earth mounds, and pyramid temples. One of the most powerful civilizations, the Maya, lasted more than 700 years. The Maya lived in

Central America in well-organized city-states, each with its own ruler who controlled trade and fought with neighboring city-states.

By around 700 the largest city in America was Teotihuacan, in central Mexico. It had more than 100,000 inhabitants and contained 600 pyramids. High up in the Andes of South America, the city of Tiahuanaco flourished between 500 and 1000.

POWERFUL CITY RULERS
A Mayan ruler, or god-king, is carried into his sacred city. Everyone had to worship him and offer tributes.

Farmers offered tributes, such as corn, to their ruler.

The Maya wore headdresses made from colorful feathers.

God-king

Priests conducted ceremonies at the top of the pyramid-temples.

THE PEOPLES OF AMERICA

As people moved south across America, many rich civilizations developed where the land was best suited for farming and settlement.

Arctic hunters

Subarctic hunters

NORTH AMERICA

Hunters and gatherers

Hopewell Indians

ATLANTIC OCEAN

MEXICO

Teotihuacan

Maya culture

CENTRAL AMERICA

PACIFIC OCEAN

Farming peoples

SOUTH AMERICA

MAYAN CITIES

The Maya built huge cities, with magnificent stone pyramid-temples. Each city-state had its own sacred city. The largest city was Tikal, in what is now Guatemala.

Pyramid-temple

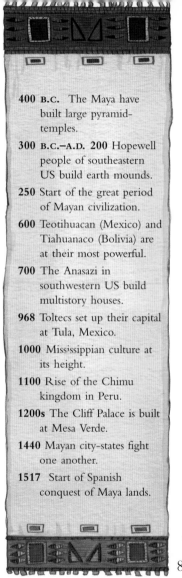

400 B.C. The Maya have built large pyramid-temples.

300 B.C.–A.D. 200 Hopewell people of southeastern US build earth mounds.

250 Start of the great period of Mayan civilization.

600 Teotihuacan (Mexico) and Tiahuanaco (Bolivia) are at their most powerful.

700 The Anasazi in southwestern US build multistory houses.

968 Toltecs set up their capital at Tula, Mexico.

1000 Mississippian culture at its height.

1100 Rise of the Chimu kingdom in Peru.

1200s The Cliff Palace is built at Mesa Verde.

1440 Mayan city-states fight one another.

1517 Start of Spanish conquest of Maya lands.

81

CHARLEMAGNE

Charles I, King of the Franks, was known as Charlemagne (Charles the Great). He founded the Holy Roman Empire and was regarded by many people as the ideal ruler. After the death of his father, Pepin the Short, and of his elder brother Carloman, Charlemagne took sole control of the Frankish Empire. He had learned much from his ruthless warrior father. He led his armies into what are now the Netherlands, Germany, and Italy. His position as Europe's strongest leader was recognized in 800 when the pope crowned him Holy Roman emperor.

AN IMPERIAL TOMB
Charlemagne's tomb, in the capital at Aachen, dates from 1215. It is decorated with gold and precious stones.

SYMBOL OF POWER
The iron lance of the Holy Roman emperors was a holy relic as well as a symbol of power.

CHARLEMAGNE THE SCHOLAR

Although Charlemagne was uneducated, he had great respect for scholarship. His capital at Aachen, with its splendid palace, was the glittering center of his empire. Charlemagne spoke Latin and Greek, had books read aloud to him and invited famous scholars to his court.

CHARLEMAGNE'S EMPIRE
The orange area shows the empire that Charlemagne inherited from his father and, later, his brother. The Frankish Empire was at its biggest extent soon after (orange and red areas).

742 Probable date of birth of Charlemagne.

752 Anointed king with brother Carloman by the pope.

768 Charlemagne's father, Pepin the Short, dies.

771 Charlemagne becomes sole ruler of the Franks.

772 Charlemagne starts war with the Saxons and converts them to Christianity.

778 Frankish army invades Spain to fight Muslims.

800 Charlemagne is crowned Emperor of the West by Pope Leo III on Christmas Day.

804 Last of Charlemagne's 18 campaigns against the Saxons.

814 Charlemagne dies. The empire grows weak.

817 The empire is split between Charlemagne's three grandsons.

THE KHMER EMPIRE

Between the ninth and the fifteenth centuries, the Khmer Empire of Cambodia dominated Southeast Asia. The Khmers were highly skilled builders and engineers, constructing cities with massive temple complexes, palaces, lakes, and canals. The Khmer Empire was created by Jayavarman I, who united people living in what are now parts of Cambodia, Thailand, Laos, and Vietnam. He and his successors were worshipped as gods. The empire reached its height in the reign of Jayavarman VII (1181–1220)—a time of energetic construction of roads, hospitals, and temples.

ANGKOR WAT
The Temple of Angkor Wat (about 1113 to 1150) is the largest of the temples built in the Khmer lands. It was dedicated to the Hindu god, Vishnu.

The central towers rose to a height of 210 feet.

Water-filled moat

The temples were carved out of sandstone.

CARVED RECORDS

Stone carvings in the ruins of Angkor Wat and in the city of Angkor Thom record the everyday activities of the Khmer people, their sacred stories, and their battle victories. Angkor was abandoned to the jungle when the Khmers were overrun by the Thais during the 1400s.

At the height of their power, the Khmer rulers controlled much of the area that is now Laos, Thailand, and Vietnam.

WAR ELEPHANTS
Trumpeting elephants with archers on their backs caused panic among the Khmers' enemies in battle.

802 King Jayavarman I founds the Khmer Empire.

900 Early stages of building the city of Angkor Thom.

1113–1150 Construction of the temple of Angkor Wat.

1181–1220 Reign of King Jayavarman VII (to 1220).

1300s Khmer Empire is weakened by costly building schemes, quarrels within the royal family, and wars with the Thais.

1431 Thai army captures Angkor. End of the Khmer Empire. A smaller Khmer kingdom lasts until 1863, when the French take control of Cambodia and Angkor Wat is rediscovered.

THE VIKINGS

The Viking homelands in Scandinavia (Norway, Sweden, and Denmark) had mountains and forests, but little good farmland. Most Vikings lived near the sea, tending fields of cereal crops and vegetables. They kept cattle and sheep, and caught fish in the rivers and fjords. Farmers made most of their household items, including tools, clothes, and furniture, out of materials such as wood, leather, and bone. Traders traveled to market towns to sell furs, reindeer antlers, and walrus ivory in exchange for weapons, jewels, and pottery.

Antler skate

Wooden bucket

Leather shoe

Iron knife

Carved stone

Goods were taken by boat to market towns.

Farmers grew vegetables such as turnips and carrots.

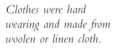
Pottery dish

IN SEARCH OF LAND AND RICHES

The Vikings grew rich through trade and agriculture and as the population increased, farmland became increasingly scarce. From the late 700s, the Vikings began to search for better farmland and more riches. They set sail from their Scandinavian homelands to raid the coasts and rivers of Europe.

VIKING LIFE

Many Vikings lived on small farms, often near rivers or the sea. They planted crops and kept animals. Viking houses were made of wood, stone, or turf, with a hole in the roof to let out smoke from the fire.

Clothes were hard wearing and made from woolen or linen cloth.

Wool tunic fastened by brooch.

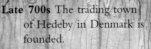

Late 700s The trading town of Hedeby in Denmark is founded.

841 Vikings found Dublin on east coast of Ireland.

850 Probable date of the Oseberg ship burial in Norway.

c. 860 Vikings begin to settle in the Baltic region.

c. 861 Ingolf is the first Viking to reach Iceland.

862 Vikings invited to rule Slavic and Finnish peoples of north Russia.

874 First Viking settlers reach Iceland.

982 Erik the Red founds settlement in Greenland.

c. 1000 Erik's son, Leif Eriksson, lands in North America and calls the new land Vinland.

1000 Jorvik (York) prospers as England's biggest Viking settlement.

1030 King Olaf the Holy converts Norway to Christianity.

1100s Swedish Vikings give up their gods and convert to Christianity.

VIKING RAIDERS

From the late 700s, bands of Vikings sailed overseas in their longships, landing on the coasts of western Europe. They raided monasteries and towns, carrying off slaves and booty, and seized land. From 865 Vikings from Denmark settled in eastern England. They attacked what is now France, but were bought off with the gift of Normandy in 911. Norwegian Vikings settled in Iceland and Greenland, and landed in North America. Vikings wandered in the markets of Baghdad and Constantinople, bringing back exotic goods to towns such as Jorvik (York) and Dublin.

Viking warrior

Chain-mail tunic

Iron sword

Leather shield

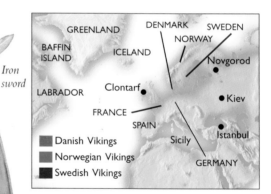

GREENLAND
DENMARK
SWEDEN
BAFFIN ISLAND
NORWAY
ICELAND
Novgorod
LABRADOR
Clontarf
Kiev
FRANCE
SPAIN
Istanbul
Sicily
GERMANY

Danish Vikings
Norwegian Vikings
Swedish Vikings

VIKING TRADE ROUTES
The Vikings traveled by sea and overland to England and Ireland in the west, and as far east as Baghdad and Istanbul.

VIKING INFLUENCE

Many Vikings were peaceful farmers and traders who chose to settle in the new lands, mingling with the local people. In England, King Alfred defeated the invaders, but Viking settlements in eastern England (the Danelaw) left a permanent legacy in customs, laws, place names, and language.

A VIKING RAID

The Vikings were fierce fighters with their favorite iron swords and axes. During an attack, raiders would rush from their longships. The ships could be rowed up rivers and land on beaches, so Vikings often took their enemies by surprise.

Iron ax

The heavy Viking sword was swung in a wide arc.

Oared longship

787 First reported Viking raids on English coast.

795 Vikings begin attacks on Ireland.

834 Vikings raid Dorestad (the Netherlands).

865 Great army of Vikings lands in England.

866 Vikings capture the city of York (Jorvik) in England.

878 English and Vikings agree to divide England between them after Vikings are defeated by King Alfred.

911 Vikings are given Normandy to prevent further attacks on France.

1016–1035 Reign of Canute, Viking king of England, Denmark, and Norway.

1066 Last big Viking attack on England, by Harold Hardrada of Norway.

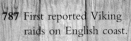

89

MEDIEVAL MONASTERIES

In medieval Europe thousands of men and women devoted their lives to the Church. These monks and nuns worked, prayed, and studied in monasteries and nunneries, which became important centers of art and learning. The head of the monastery was the abbot. The head of a nunnery, a religious house for women, was called an abbess. Men and women who became monks or nuns followed a strict way of life. They had to be poor, unmarried, and obedient. Their program of prayer and worship included eight services every day.

Chapel

The monks cared for the sick in the infirmary.

Dormitory

A MONASTIC
COMMUNITY
Monks followed a daily routine of work and worship. At the heart of every monastery was the chapel. There were also herb gardens and cloisters, an infirmary, workshops, and farm buildings.

Cloisters

*Refectory
(dining hall)*

Kitchen

MONKS AND FRIARS

There were several organizations, or orders, of monks, including the Benedictines, Carthusians, and Cistercians. In the 1200s new orders of traveling preachers, known as friars, were formed. Friars did not live behind monastery walls, but wandered the countryside, asking for food and shelter and preaching Christianity.

Monks at prayer

ILLUMINATED BOOKS
Monks copied out books, decorating the pages with brilliantly colored letters and pictures, called illuminations. Each page took hours of work.

Library

Vegetable garden

Late 400s Simple monasteries are founded in Ireland, for groups of hermits.

529 St. Benedict of Nursia founds the first order of monks.

500s St. Columba founds a monastery on the island of Iona.

529 First European abbey at Monte Cassino in Italy is founded.

597 St. Augustine founds the first English Benedictine monastery at Canterbury.

966 Benedictines build Mont St. Michel in France.

1084 Order of Carthusians is founded.

1098 Cistercian order is founded.

1100 First monastery founded by the Knights of St. John to shelter Holy Land pilgrims.

Late 1100s University of Paris is founded.

1249 First college of Oxford University is founded.

MEDIEVAL CASTLES

Mighty stone castles dotted the landscape of
Europe and the Middle East throughout the
Middle Ages. The earliest castles were built by
the Norman invaders of England. They were
earth mounds, often built on hilltops, with a
wooden stockade on top. The castles were soon enlarged and
strengthened, with water-filled ditches or moats, stone walls
protected by towers, and a massive central stronghold called a
keep. Medieval castles were private fortresses for the king or
lord who owned them. A castle was also a family home,
although early castles were cold and drafty places.

CASTLE DEFENSES

The castle was defended by foot soldiers with spears and
bows and by armored knights on horseback. When a
castle was attacked, its walls had to be thick enough
to withstand catapults, tunnels, and battering
rams. The occupants often suffered from
starvation or disease, and were forced
to surrender.

Musicians

*Dancers
entertained
the feasting
family.*

FEASTING IN THE GREAT HALL
The lord and his followers feasted in the great hall.
The lord and lady sat on a raised dais, and knights
and other members of the household at lower tables.

Servants carried in food from the kitchen.

Jousters

JOUSTING KNIGHTS
Jousting was combat on horseback between knights with blunt lances. It was a popular social occasion.

Dogs scavenged for scraps.

500 Byzantines build strong stone castles and walled cities.

800s Arabs build castles in the Middle East and North Africa.

1000s Normans develop the motte (mound) and bailey (enclosure) castle.

1078 William I begins building the Tower of London, England.

1100s Stone keeps become the main castle stronghold.

1180s Castles with square-walled towers are built.

1200s The concentric or ring-wall castle is developed.

1220s Castles with round-walled towers start to be built.

1280s Edward I of England orders a chain of great castles to be built in England and Wales.

1350s Castles made of brick are built in the Netherlands and England.

93

MEDIEVAL TOWNS

In the Middle Ages, towns in Europe were noisy and crowded by day, but quiet and dark at night. Houses were built close together, with the top floors often jutting out over the street.

Many houses were also shops and workplaces. You took care where you walked in a medieval town, because most people threw their rubbish into the street. Open drains ran alongside and smelled awful.

A MEDIEVAL MARKET
On market day, people brought in farm produce to sell, spent their money at stalls and shops, and drank at the ale house.

Farmers sold their produce.

Entertainers kept the crowds amused.

Inn

Juggler

Dancing bear

SPRINGTIME WORK
This page, entitled "March," is from a fifteenth-century illuminated manuscript. The farmer in the foreground is plowing. Shepherds, peasants, and other farm workers are busy with springtime tasks.

BUSY TOWN LIFE

Churches, guilds, fairs, and markets all drew people into the towns. Groups called guilds were formed by traders and craftworkers to organize their businesses and to set standards of work. Guilds also staged pageants, dramas, and religious processions, and set up training schools. Some towns were famous for their fairs and attracted foreign merchants from all over Europe, as well as entertainers. Work was also to be found in towns building magnificent cathedrals and churches, as well as castles and defensive walls.

WILLIAM, DUKE OF NORMANDY, the first Norman king of England. He was crowned in Westminster Abbey on Christmas Day, 1066.

EUROPEAN MERCHANTS carried heavy metal coins. Italian merchants set up banks, using written bills of exchange instead of coins.

PEASANTS in the Middle Ages worked on land owned by the local lord. In return for their loyalty, he protected them.

PILGRIMS made journeys to visit holy places or shrines. Chaucer wrote about a group of pilgrims in his *Canterbury Tales.*

THE CRUSADES

A Crusader knight

For European Christians, the Crusades were holy wars, with the promise of plunder. For more than 200 years, Christian and Muslim armies fought for control of territory around Jerusalem known as the Holy Land. Jerusalem was a holy city to Jews, Muslims, and Christians but, in 1095, the Muslim Turks banned Christian pilgrims from the city. This angered both the western Christian Church in Rome and the eastern Christian Church in Constantinople. Christians were called upon to free Jerusalem and so launched the First Crusade, or war of the cross.

Steep ramparts

ATTACK!
Once Crusaders had conquered lands, they built strong castles to defend them.

Battering rams broke down walls.

96

A Muslim warrior

SUCCESS AND FAILURE

The Crusades inspired stories of bravery and honor. Crusaders had to be tough to endure difficult conditions on their journey. In 1099 the army of the First Crusade captured Jerusalem. Yet none of the later crusades matched this initial success, and the Crusaders failed to win back the Holy Land.

Giant catapults threw balls of flaming tar.

Boiling oil was poured on attackers.

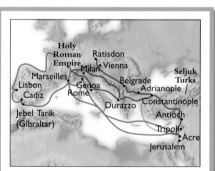

TO THE HOLY LAND
This map shows the different route to Jerusalem taken by the First Crusade (blue), the Second Crusade (yellow), and the Third Crusade (red).

1096 First Crusade is called by Pope Urban II.

1099 The Crusaders defeat the Turks and capture Jerusalem.

1147 Second Crusade sets out.

1187 Muslim leader Saladin captures Jerusalem.

1189 Third Crusade is led by Frederick I Barbarossa of the Holy Roman Empire, Philip II of France, and Richard I of England.

1202 Fourth Crusade attacks Egypt.

1221 Fifth Crusade fights the Sultan of Egypt.

1228 The Sixth Crusade ends when Muslims hand over Jerusalem.

1244 Muslims retake Jerusalem.

1249 Seventh Crusade is led by King Louis IX of France.

1270 Eighth Crusade also led by Louis. He and many of his men die of plague in Tunis.

THE MONGOL EMPIRE

In the 1200s, Mongol armies sent a shockwave of fear around Asia and Europe, conquering a vast area of land that formed the largest empire in history.

The Mongols were nomads living on the plains of central Asia. In 1206, Chief Temujin brought all the tribes under his rule and was proclaimed Genghis Khan, meaning lord of all.

WANDERING NOMADS
The Mongols searched for fresh grassland for their herds, carrying their portable felt homes, called yurts, with them.

WARRIORS ON HORSEBACK
Mongol warriors fought on horseback. They controlled their horses with their feet, leaving their hands free to shoot bows and hurl spears.

Bow

Mongol soldiers were expert archers.

Spear

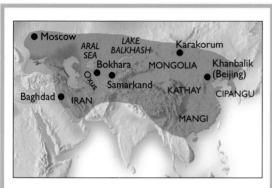

THE WORLD'S LARGEST EMPIRE
Although ruthless in battle, Genghis Khan kept peace
in his empire. It stretched from the River Danube in
the west to the Pacific shores of Asia in the east.

MONGOL CONQUESTS

The Mongols quickly conquered the Persian
Empire. They continued their attacks after
Genghis Khan died and, in 1237, a Mongol
army led by Batu Khan, one of Genghis's sons,
invaded Russia. Western Europe was saved only
when the Mongols turned homeward on the
death of Ogodai Khan in 1241. Enemies feared
the Mongols' speed and ferocity in battle. In
victory, the Mongols were usually merciless,
slaughtering people and plundering treasure.
Yet they ruled their empire fairly if sternly.

1206 Temujin becomes
chief of all the
Mongols, taking the
name Genghis Khan.

1215 Beijing, capital of
China, is taken by
the Mongols.

1217 The Mongols
control all China and
Korea.

1219 The Mongols attack
the empire of
Khwarezm (Persia
and Turkey).

1224 Mongol armies
invade Russia,
Poland, and Hungary.

1227 Genghis Khan dies.

1229 Genghis's son,
Ogodai, becomes
khan.

1237 Mongol army
known as the
Golden Horde
invades northern
Russia.

1241 Ogodai dies and
his armies pull back
from Europe.

KUBLAI KHAN AND CHINA

Kublai Khan, grandson of Genghis Khan, became leader of the Mongols in 1260. His armies moved from the windswept steppes of central Asia to overthrow the Song Dynasty in China, and by 1279 he controlled most of this vast country. At this time, China was the world's most sophisticated, technologically advanced country. The new Mongol emperor moved his capital to Beijing, taking care to maintain many aspects of Chinese culture. Chinese silks, porcelain, and other luxuries astonished travelers from Europe and Africa. After Kublai Khan's death, the Mongol Empire declined and had largely broken up by the mid-1300s.

ALONG THE SILK ROAD
Merchants traveled in caravans for protection against bandits. From China, they followed the Silk Road across mountains and deserts to the markets of the Middle East.

Camels laden with Chinese goods.

Travelers rested at caravanserai, or rest stations.

MARCO POLO (1256–1323)
The Italian explorer Marco Polo toured
China in the service of Kublai Khan.

A SOPHISTICATED NATION

After visiting Kublai Khan's court, Marco Polo wrote in praise of Chinese cities, China's fine postal system, and its paper money. The Chinese had discovered technologies such as paper-making. Other inventions included the magnetic compass and exploding gunpowder rockets.

EARLY PAPER

The Chinese began making paper in about 105. They used hemp or tree bark for fiber. Later, they mashed rags or old rope into pulp.

Pulp was spread on mesh trays to dry into sheets.

1216 Kublai Khan is born.

1260 Kublai is elected Great Khan of the Mongols.

1271 Marco Polo sets out from Venice for China.

1274 Kublai Khan sends an army to invade Japan, but it is driven back by a storm.

1276 Mongols defeat the Song fleet near Guangzhou.

1279 Kublai Khan rules all China.

1294 Kublai Khan dies.

1368 Mongols are driven from China by Ming forces.

1395 Tamerlane, a descendant of Genghis Khan, invades large parts of southern Russia.

1398 Tamerlane invades Delhi, India.

1405 Tamerlane dies.

THE BLACK DEATH

The Black Death was the most horrific natural disaster of the Middle Ages. It was a devastating plague that killed many millions of people in Europe and Asia. In 1347, Italian sailors arriving in Europe from Asia brought disease with them. The disease was bubonic plague, which passed to humans from infected rats through flea bites. The name "Black Death" came from the black spots that appeared on victims, who also developed swellings and coughed up blood. No medieval doctor knew why the Black Death struck or how to cure it.

MEDIEVAL DEATH
Many people fled from their homes, leaving the sick to die. Houses were marked with crosses to show where the disease had struck.

Crosses marked diseased homes.

The dead were carried away in carts for burial.

SPREADING THE PLAGUE

As the epidemic spread at terrifying speed, panic-stricken people fled from the towns. They took the plague with them into the surrounding countryside. Around 20 million people in Europe alone may have died from the Black Death.

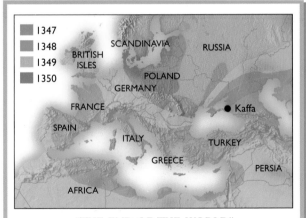

1347
1348
1349
1350

SCANDINAVIA
RUSSIA
BRITISH ISLES
POLAND
GERMANY
FRANCE
● Kaffa
SPAIN
ITALY
TURKEY
GREECE
PERSIA
AFRICA

"THE END OF THE WORLD"
This map shows how the Black Death spread, raging from China across to Scandinavia. One Italian historian wrote: "This is the end of the world."

1344 Bubonic plague breaks out in China and India.

1347 The plague reaches Genoa in Italy and spreads west across Europe.

1348 The disease starts to kill people in southern England.

1349 Black Death spreads to Ireland, Wales, and Scotland. Other regions affected include France, Spain, Germany, and Russia.

1350 The epidemic reaches Scandinavia.

1353 Black Death epidemic eases. As many as 20 million people in Europe are dead.

1400 Further outbreaks of the Black Death continue until this date.

AFRICAN KINGDOMS

In this period, the riches of the mightiest kingdoms in Africa impressed Muslim and European visitors. In the kingdom of Ghana (modern-day Gambia, Guinea, Mali, and Senegal), traders marveled at warriors with gold-mounted swords and shields guarding the king. Ghana reached the peak of its power in the 10th century when it controlled both the gold and salt trade.

FROM MALI TO MECCA
Mansa Musa, ruler of the Mali Empire, made a pilgrimage to Mecca in 1324, with an entourage of 60,000 followers.

TRADE WITHOUT MONEY
*Traders used cowrie shells, like these strung on
a cord, as currency. They also bartered,
exchanging goods of equal value.*

TRADING NATIONS

In the 1300s, the Islamic kingdom of Mali
replaced Ghana as West Africa's most powerful
empire. The fame of Mali's
most famous ruler, Mansa
Musa, spread to Europe.
His kingdom was shown
on maps as a land
glittering with gold.
Farther south, trade in
the kingdoms of Ife and
Benin made powerful rulers

MALI

GHANA

rich. The people of Benin traded with the
Portuguese when their ships began sailing
along the West African coast in the 1400s.

BRONZES FROM BENIN
*The craftworkers of Africa were skilled in metalworking.
This bronze hand altar shows a Benin king with his
wives, servants and soldiers. Craftworkers in Benin made
high-quality cast bronze figures, the finest metal sculptures
in Africa.*

770 In West Africa, Soninke
people begin to build the
kingdom of Ghana.

800 Ife kingdom in Nigeria
and Kanem–Bornu (north
of Lake Chad) become
prominent.

800s Arabs and Persians set
up trading posts in
East Africa.

900s Ghana controls gold and
salt trade and also buys
cloth from Europe.

999 Baganda is first king of
Kano in western Nigeria.

1043 Mandingo Empire of
Jenne founded in
West Africa.

1200s Founding of Benin
kingdom under the first
oba (ruler), Eweka.

1240 Ghana becomes part of
the new Mali Empire.

1307 Mali Empire at its
height, with its capital
at Timbuktu.

1332 Probable year of Mansa
Musa's death.

1440–1480 Reign of the most
famous oba of Benin,
Ewuare the Great.

THE HUNDRED YEARS WAR

Edward III became king of England in 1327. He believed he also had a claim to the French throne so in 1337, he declared war on France. War between England and France lasted on and off until 1453.

Edward's forces won a sea battle and two great land victories at Crécy and Poitiers, but were driven back by the French king Charles V. In 1360 Edward gave up his claim to the French throne in return for land.

Soldiers fought with a longbow, primitive cannon, and crossbow.

The English hoped Joan of Arc's death would end French resistance.

Years of truce followed until the English king Henry V renewed his claim to the throne in 1414. He led his troops to France, where they defeated a much larger French army at Agincourt in 1415. To make peace Henry then married the French king's daughter, but he died in 1422 before his baby son could become king of France. The fighting continued as the French were inspired by a peasant girl named Joan of Arc (1412–1431). She fought until the English caught her and burned her at the stake. Under the weak rule of Henry VI, the English lost ground and by 1453, they had lost all French territory except Calais.

1337 Edward III goes to war with France, claiming the throne.

1340 Sea battle of Sluys (off Belgium) won by the English.

1356 Poitiers is a victory for the English led by Edward III's son, the Black Prince.

1380 Death of Charles V of France who was succeeded by the mad Charles VI.

1415 Victory at Agincourt gives Henry V control of France.

1420 Henry V marries Catherine, daughter of Charles VI.

1422 Henry V dies.

1431 Joan of Arc is burned to death.

1453 End of the Hundred Years War.

THE AGE OF DISCOVERY

Explorers and empires 1400–1700

The 1400s mark the end of the Middle Ages. In Europe, the new ideas of the Renaissance and Reformation transformed the way people thought about themselves and the world, and the way they lived. Three events are often picked out as marking the end of the medieval period and the start of the modern age. They are the fall of Constantinople in 1453, which ended the last traces of the old Roman empire; the development of printing in the

1450s, which made books available to anyone who could read; and the first voyage of Christopher Columbus to the Americas in 1492.

This period also marks a time when the peoples of the world came into increasing contact with each other. People in America, Africa and Asia had greater contact with Europe. Europeans increased their power in the world through trade, through the use of new technology such as cannons and muskets, and through a restless search for new lands and wealth.

THE RENAISSANCE

The Renaissance was a rebirth of interest in the art and learning of ancient Greece and Rome. Many historians say that it marked the beginning of our modern world. The Renaissance began in the fourteenth century in the universities and monasteries of northern Italy, and spread throughout Europe. People rediscovered Latin and Greek manuscripts on science, art, and literature. The new technology of printing with movable type, developed by

ITALIAN MASTERPIECE
The great dome of Florence Cathedral in Italy was designed by Filippo Brunelleschi, the first major architect of the Italian Renaissance.

THE NEW UNIVERSE
The Polish astronomer Copernicus put forward a revolutionary new theory in 1543. He suggested that the Sun, not the Earth, lies at the center of the universe. This challenged the established theory of the Greek astronomer Ptolemy.

Johannes Gutenberg in Germany, made books cheaper and more plentiful. New ideas could now be read by many more people. The Renaissance changed the Western world forever.

NEW TECHNOLOGY
A print workshop in Denmark, about 1600. The technology of printing with a screw press and metal type spread throughout Europe.

1308 Dante Alighieri begins writing *The Divine Comedy.*

1387 Geoffrey Chaucer begins *The Canterbury Tales.*

1454 Johannes Gutenberg prints with movable type. By 1476 William Caxton is printing in London.

1466–1536 Life of Desiderius Erasmus, a Dutch scholar, philosopher, and writer.

1478 Lorenzo de Medici makes Florence a center of art and learning.

1503 The rebuilding of St. Peter's in Rome begins. Leonardo da Vinci paints the *Mona Lisa.*

1508 Michelangelo paints the ceiling of the Sistine Chapel in the Vatican, Rome.

1532 Hans Holbein, Flemish artist, is at work in England.

1543 Copernicus puts forward his ideas about the universe.

111

EMPIRES OF THE SUN

Two civilizations reached their peak during the early 1500s—the Aztecs in Central America and the Incas in South America. The empires of both civilizations eventually fell to Spanish rule. The Aztecs were fierce warriors whose empire stretched across Mexico. They were skilled sculptors, poets, musicians, and engineers, but in 1521 they lost their empire to Spanish treasure-seekers.

THE END OF AN EMPIRE
The Spanish were vastly outnumbered in their battles with the Incas. But the Europeans had horses and guns, both new to the Incas. When the Inca ruler Atahualpa was killed, the leaderless Inca armies were quickly defeated.

Spanish soldier on horseback.

The Inca armies were weak after seven years of civil war.

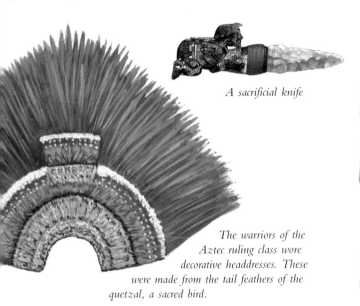

A sacrificial knife

The warriors of the Aztec ruling class wore decorative headdresses. These were made from the tail feathers of the quetzal, a sacred bird.

THE INCAS OF PERU

From the mountains of Peru, the god-emperor of the Incas ruled a highly organized empire. The Inca ruler Pachacuti and his successors increased the empire to include parts of Chile, Bolivia, and Ecuador. The Incas built stone cities, such as their capital at Cuzco, and fine roads for trade. In the 1530s a small Spanish expedition under Francisco Pizarro arrived to seek gold in South America. The Spanish killed the emperor Atahualpa and defeated his armies, causing the empire to fall.

1325 The Aztec capital of Tenochtitlan is founded.

1438 Inca Empire starts, under Pachacuti.

1440–1469 Reign of Montezuma I.

1450–1500 The Inca Empire is extended into modern-day Bolivia, Chile, Ecuador and Colombia.

1519 Hernando Cortés leads Spanish soldiers into Tenochtitlan. Montezuma welcomes them, believing Cortés is the god Quetzalcoatl.

1520 The Aztecs rise up against the Spanish. Montezuma dies.

1521 Cortés captures Tenochtitlan, ending the Aztec Empire.

1527 Death of the Inca emperor Huayna Capac; civil war starts between his sons.

1532 Francisco Pizarro, with 167 soldiers, attacks Inca forces and captures Cuzco.

113

VOYAGES OF DISCOVERY

In the late 1400s and 1500s, Europeans set out to explore the oceans. Building stronger ships capable of longer voyages, they went in search of trade, new lands, and treasure. The Portuguese, under Prince Henry the Navigator, were the first to go exploring. They sailed along the west coast of Africa, trading in gold and ivory. Spanish, French, Dutch, and English sailors followed. Some sailed west to find a route to India. Christopher Columbus was the first fifteenth-century explorer to cross the Atlantic and return.

Peppers

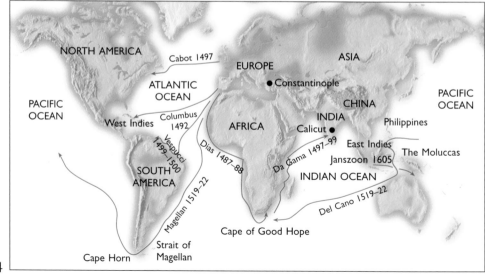

NORTH AMERICA

Cabot 1497

EUROPE

ASIA

● Constantinople

ATLANTIC OCEAN

PACIFIC OCEAN

CHINA

PACIFIC OCEAN

West Indies

Columbus 1492

INDIA

Calicut ●

Philippines

AFRICA

Vespucci 1499–1500

Dias 1487–88

Da Gama 1497–99

East Indies

The Moluccas

Janszoon 1605

SOUTH AMERICA

INDIAN OCEAN

Del Cano 1519–22

Magellan 1519–22

Cape of Good Hope

Cape Horn

Strait of Magellan

Potatoes

NEW WORLD FOODS
European explorers brought back new foods, such as potatoes, tomatoes, and peppers. Chocolate was first brought to Spain from Mexico in 1520.

Tomatoes

AROUND THE WORLD

The explorers' ships were small, using a mixture of square and lateen (triangular) sails for easier steering and greater maneuverability. Sailors had only crude maps and simple instruments to guide them. In 1519 Ferdinand Magellan sailed from Spain with five ships. Only one ship returned after completing the first round-the-world voyage.

EARLY NAVIGATION
Navigators used the cross staff and astrolabe to fix their ships' position by the Sun and stars. The magnetic compass pointed North, but was not always reliable.

Compass

Cross staff

Astrolabe

1419 Portuguese sail to the Madeira Islands.

1431 Portuguese reach the Azores.

1488 Bartolomeu Dias of Portugal explores west coast of Africa.

1492 Christopher Columbus makes his first voyage to America with three ships.

1497 John Cabot, an Italian in the service of England, sails to Canada. The Portuguese explorer Vasco Da Gama sails round Africa to India.

1501 Italian Amerigo Vespucci sails to South America.

1517 Portuguese traders reach China.

1522 First round-the-world voyage is completed by Ferdinand Magellan's Spanish crew.

SPAIN AND PORTUGAL

Spain became the superpower of Europe in the 1500s. Medieval Spain was divided between Christian and Muslim kingdoms. However, in 1469 the marriage of two Christian monarchs, Ferdinand of Aragon and Isabella of Castile, united Spain's strongest Christian kingdoms and ended Muslim rule. The new rulers set up the Spanish Inquisition to search out heretics—people who held different beliefs from the established Church. Spain's power was based on a strong army and a large navy, which controlled the gold and silver trade from the Americas.

King Philip II ruled 1556–1598.

COLUMBUS SAILS TO AMERICA
This painting shows Columbus leaving the Spanish court, having won the support of Ferdinand and Isabella for his westward voyage.

BUILDING AN EMPIRE

By 1580, the Spanish Empire included Portugal. With its long coastline and shipbuilding skills, Portugal had led the way in European exploration of the oceans. The Portuguese controlled large stretches of coastline in East and West Africa, Brazil, and India, as well as trading posts in India and China.

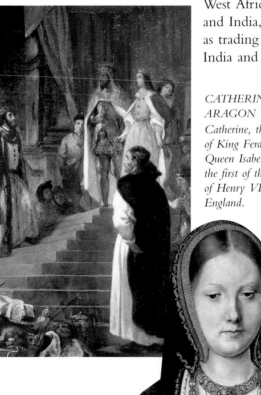

CATHERINE OF ARAGON
Catherine, the daughter of King Ferdinand and Queen Isabella, became the first of the six wives of Henry VIII of England.

1385 Henry the Navigator begins Portugal's rise as a sea power.

1479 Christian kingdoms of Aragon and Castile are united.

1492 Moors are forced out of Granada. Jews are expelled from Spain. Columbus sails to America.

1512 Ferdinand seizes Navarre to complete unification of Spain.

1516–1556 Reign of Charles I.

1521 Spain conquers Aztec Empire in Mexico.

1535 Spain conquers Inca Empire of Peru.

1556 Philip II becomes king of Spain.

1568 War in the Spanish Netherlands begins.

1580 Spain conquers Portugal and holds it until 1640.

1588 Spanish Armada fails to invade England.

117

AFRICAN EMPIRES

Africa in 1500 was a continent with many kingdoms and empires, its richest rulers trading in gold, ivory, and slaves—goods that attracted European traders. The strongest empire was Songhai, a Muslim kingdom that controlled trade across the Sahara Desert. Another Muslim empire was Kanem–Bornu, which thrived on trade between northern and southern Africa. To the east, the Christian empire of Ethiopia lay in the heart of Muslim Africa.

TRADE IN TIMBUKTU
Traders do business in the city of Timbuktu, the center of the gold and salt trade.

Merchants brought cloth from Morocco.

Gold and ivory were traded.

GREAT ZIMBABWE

The settlement at Great Zimbabwe in southern Africa was built over a period of about 400 years. The walled citadel of Great Zimbabwe was used by rulers as a stronghold and administrative center. By 1450 this prosperous African kingdom was a major religious, political, and trading center. Its people used copper and iron, and traded in gold. By 1500 the civilization that built Zimbabwe was in decline.

KINGDOMS OF AFRICA
This map shows the most important African kingdoms during the 1400s and 1500s.

PRESTER JOHN
Travelers told of a legendary Christian ruler called Prester ("priest") John. He was first said to be an Asian king, and later the ruler of Ethiopia.

1335 The Songhai ruling dynasty is founded.

1430s Portuguese begin exploring the west coast of Africa.

1450 Kingdom of Great Zimbabwe is at its greatest extent.

1464 Songhai breaks away from Mali's control.

1493 Askia Muhammad I heads new ruling dynasty in Songhai, now at its peak.

1506 The kingdom of Kongo has its first Christian king, Afonso I.

c. 1530 The transatlantic slave trade from Africa to the Americas begins.

1571–1603 Idris Alawma rules the empire of Kanem-Bornu.

1591 Songhai Empire is defeated by Moroccan, Spanish, and Portuguese soldiers.

THE REFORMATION

The Reformation was a challenge to the established Christian Church in western Europe. It was based on a new philosophy called humanism—the belief that people controlled their own destinies. In 1517 Martin Luther, a German monk, protested at what he saw as the Church's theological corruption. His campaign for reform started the Reformation and resulted in the creation of the Protestant Church. The new technology of printing helped to spread these new ideas, and for the first time the Bible was translated from Latin into local languages for all to read.

English fleet launches its fireships to attack the Spanish.

HENRY VIII OF ENGLAND
Henry VIII used discontent with the Church to his advantage. To gain a divorce, he broke with the Catholic Church and became head of the Church of England.

THE COUNTER REFORMATION

From 1545, the Catholic Church fought back with a movement known as the Counter Reformation, sending out Jesuit priests to campaign against the spread of Protestantism. The split between Christians in western Europe led to wars, and Catholics and Protestants persecuted one another, often in the cruelest ways.

THE SPANISH ARMADA

In 1588 the Spanish sent the Armada against England to restore Catholic rule. An English fireship attack helped fight off the invasion, and storms eventually wrecked the Spanish fleet.

Spanish warship

Warships were powered by oars and sails.

1517 Martin Luther protests church corruption.

1519 Ulrich Zwingli starts the Reformation in Switzerland.

1529 Henry VIII breaks with Rome, divorces Catherine of Aragon.

1532 John Calvin starts Protestant movement in France.

1534 Henry VIII is head of the Church of England.

1541 John Knox takes the Reformation to Scotland.

1555 England returns to Catholicism under Mary I.

1558–1603 Elizabeth I, a Protestant, rules England.

1562 Religious wars in France between Catholics and Protestant Huguenots.

1588 Defeat of the Spanish Armada.

1598 French Catholics and Protestants are given equal rights.

OTTOMANS AND SAFAVIDS

The Ottoman capture of Constantinople in 1453 marked the beginning of a Turkish golden age. The Ottomans fought many wars against their Muslim rivals in Persia, the Safavids. Constantinople, renamed Istanbul, became the center of a vast Muslim empire. Most conquests were made during the rule of Suleiman I. The Ottoman advance into Europe was checked when the Turkish army failed to capture Vienna in 1529. Ottoman galleys (oared warships) controlled the Mediterranean Sea, but in 1571 the Turkish fleet was defeated by a Christian fleet at Lepanto.

PERSIAN CARPETS
Persian spinners and weavers made famous carpets of knotted wool and silk. They featured soft colors and elegant patterns.

SULEIMAN THE MAGNIFICENT
The Ottoman ruler Suleiman I made the Ottoman Empire a power to be respected and feared in the Middle East and in Europe.

EMPIRES AT WAR

The Ottoman sultan Suleiman tried three times to conquer Persia, which from 1501 was ruled by the Safavid Dynasty. Here the people were Shiites, not Sunni Muslims as in the Ottoman Empire. Safavid rivalry with the Ottomans continued, and wars between the two empires helped to stop the Ottomans advancing into Europe.

Budapest
BLACK SEA   **CASPIAN SEA**
Constantinople   *Baku*
MEDITERRANEAN SEA   *Tehran*
Kandahar
EGYPT
TRIPOLITANIA
ARABIA
ARABIAN SEA

IMPERIAL RULE
The map shows the Ottoman and Safavid Empires. Scholars from across the Islamic world visited the imperial rulers.

1453 Ottomans capture the city of Constantinople.

1501 Foundation of the Safavid Dynasty in Persia.

1516 Ottoman Turks conquer Egypt.

1520–1566 Suleiman I rules the Ottoman Empire.

1529 At the siege of Vienna, the Turks fail to capture the city.

1534 Turks capture Tunis, Baghdad, and Mesopotamia.

1571 The Ottoman fleet is destroyed at the Battle of Lepanto.

1587 Shah Abbas I comes to the throne of Persia.

1590 Turks and Persians make peace.

c. 1600 The Ottoman Empire begins to decline.

123

THE MUGHALS

The Mughal Dynasty ruled a mighty empire in India for nearly 300 years. Its founder, Babur, was a shrewd and able ruler. His grandson, Akbar, was an even greater ruler, under whose reign Mughal art and learning flourished. A conqueror who crushed rebellions, Akbar was famed as a wise and just ruler. He tolerated all religions, and introduced new styles in art and architecture.

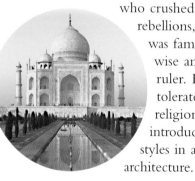

THE TAJ MAHAL, AGRA
The Taj Mahal was built for the favorite wife of Mughal emperor, Shah Jahan.

Enemy fortress

War elephants were used like tanks.

The Mughal soldiers had firearms.

124

THE DYNASTY CONTINUES

Akbar's grandson, Shah Jahan, also set about enlarging the empire. He, too, was a great patron of the arts and paid for many splendid buildings, including the Taj Mahal. Shah Jahan was imprisoned by one of his sons, Aurangzeb, who seized the throne. Shah Jahan died in captivity and was buried next to his wife in the Taj Mahal. Aurangzeb, a strict Muslim, was the last great Mughal ruler, expanding the empire to its greatest extent.

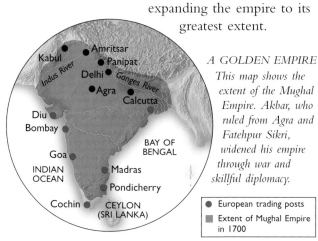

A GOLDEN EMPIRE
This map shows the extent of the Mughal Empire. Akbar, who ruled from Agra and Fatehpur Sikri, widened his empire through war and skillful diplomacy.

- ● European trading posts
- ■ Extent of Mughal Empire in 1700

AKBAR THE CONQUEROR
This 1568 painting shows Mughal soldiers storming an enemy fortress. Akbar was a great military leader whose armies defeated several Hindu kingdoms.

1526 Foundation of the Mughal Dynasty. Babur controls northern India.

1529 Akbar defeats the Afghans.

1556–1605 Reign of Akbar, grandson of Babur.

1565 Akbar extends his rule to southern India. A great fort is built at Agra.

1567 Akbar subdues the Rajput princes.

1569 Royal court of Fatehpur Sikri is founded.

1575 Akbar conquers Bengal.

1605 Jahangir succeeds Akbar

1627–1657 Rule of Shah Jahan.

1658–1707 Rule of Aurangzeb.

1720s Mughal Empire collapses.

125

MING CHINA

In 1368 a Buddhist monk named Ming Hong Wu founded the Ming Dynasty, which ruled China for almost 300 years. Under Hong Wu, China enjoyed peace and prosperity. He made Chinese society more equal by abolishing slavery, redistributing land, and demanding higher taxes from the rich. With a strong army, China reasserted its power over its neighbors. The Ming Dynasty was also a period of great artistic creativity.

JAPANESE INVADERS
Chinese soldiers fight against invading Japanese samurai. In the 1590s the Japanese tried to invade Korea, an ally of the Chinese.

Chinese soldier on horseback

An arrow fired from a powerful bow could pierce a wooden shield.

Japanese samurai warrior

A CHINESE CROSSBOW
A powerful artillery crossbow like this could fire an arrow up to 650 feet (200 m).

CONTACT WITH OUTSIDERS

China's first contacts with European traders began in the 1500s, when Portuguese ships arrived. Western traders were eager to buy Chinese porcelain and silk and a new drink, tea, which first reached Europe in 1610. The Chinese had seldom looked far beyond their borders and after the mid-1500s the government banned voyages overseas.

THE FORBIDDEN CITY
From 1421, the Ming emperors lived inside the Forbidden City in Beijing, a huge complex of palaces, temples, and parks into which no foreigner was admitted.

1368 The Ming Dynasty is founded.

1398 Death of the first Ming emperor, Hong Wu.

1405–1433 Admiral Zheng He leads seven voyages to explore India and East Africa.

1421 The capital moves from Nanjing to Beijing.

1514 Portuguese traders arrive in China, followed by the Dutch in 1522.

1551 Chinese government bans voyages beyond Chinese waters.

1557 The Portuguese set up a trading base at Macao.

1560 Ming forces drive off Mongols and pirate raids, until peace and prosperity are restored.

1575 Spanish begin trade with China.

1592–1598 Ming armies help Koreans to fight off Japanese invaders.

1644 The last Ming emperor, Ssu Tsung, commits suicide.

TOKUGAWA JAPAN

The Tokugawa, or Edo, period brought a long period of stability and unity to Japan. In 1603 the emperor appointed Tokugawa Ieyasu to the position of shogun (a powerful military leader and effective ruler of Japan). Ieyasu, the first of the Tokugawa shoguns, ran the country on the emperor's behalf. His government centered on the fishing village of Edo, which later became known as Tokyo. Ieyasu reorganized Japan into regions called domains, each of which was led by a *daimyo* who controlled the local groups of warriors, or samurai.

SAMURAI WARRIORS
Boys trained from childhood to become warriors. Their main weapons were bows and arrows, single-edged swords, and daggers.

The Samurai fought on horseback as well as on foot.

Single-edged sword

Armor for protection

A WARLORD'S STRONGHOLD
Himeji castle was the stronghold of the warlord Hideyoshi during the civil wars that tore Japan apart.

JAPANESE ISOLATION
At first, Japan was visited by Portuguese, English, and Dutch traders. Missionaries converted many Japanese to Christianity. Ieyasu thought the new religion might undermine his rule and in 1637 missionaries were banned. Despite Japan's isolation from the rest of the world the country flourished and its population and food production increased.

A complicated hairstyle made it difficult to move the head.

JAPANESE SOCIETY
Under the strict society of the Tokugawas, wealthy women were treated as ornaments. The clothing and shoes they wore made it almost impossible to walk.

Long flowing gown

Very high shoes

1543 Birth of Tokugawa Ieyasu.

1560 Ieyasu returns to his own lands and allies himself with the warlord, Nobunaga.

1584 After several small battles, Ieyasu allies himself with the warlord Hideyoshi.

1598 After the death of Hideyoshi, Japan's warlords struggle for power.

1603 The emperor appoints Ieyasu shogun and the Tokugawa period begins.

1605 Ieyasu abdicates as shogun but continues to advise his successors.

1616 Death of Ieyasu.

1637 Christianity is banned in Japan and foreigners, except the Dutch, are forced to leave.

1830s Peasants and samurai rebel against the Tokugawas.

1867 The last Tokugawa shogun is overthrown.

OCEANIA

The people of Oceania—Australia, New Zealand, and the Pacific islands—lived by hunting and food gathering, fishing, and farming. The first aboriginal peoples of Australia probably arrived from Southeast Asia about 40,000 years ago. Their rich cultural life included the myths of the Dreamtime and ornate rock paintings. About 3,500 years ago, the ancestors of the Polynesians set sail from eastern Asia to find new lands. They reached Easter Island in the western Pacific and the Hawaiian Islands in the north.

MAORI WARRIORS
The Maoris built wooden stockades, called pas.
Warriors fought from platforms on the walls. At
sea, Maori warriors set out on raids in war canoes.

Hill fort

Wooden stockade

EASTER ISLAND
One of the mysterious stone statues on Easter Island in the Pacific. More than 600 stone statues are scattered around the island.

THE MAORIS OF NEW ZEALAND

Polynesian Maoris came to New Zealand probably in about A.D. 750. There were frequent feuds and wars between Maori groups. They built hill forts with stockades and platforms from which warriors hurled weapons at their enemies. Maoris decorated their faces and bodies with tattoos to show their rank. European explorers only reached New Zealand in 1642.

FLIGHTLESS BIRDS
The flightless moas that lived in New Zealand died out in the 1700s.

A Maori war canoe sets out on a raid.

Wooden war canoe

c. 400 First settlers land on Easter Island.

c. 750 Maoris start to settle New Zealand by this time.

1300 All New Zealand is settled. Huge stone statues are erected on Easter Island.

1526 Portuguese land on Papua New Guinea.

1567 Spanish explorer Mendana de Neyra visits the Solomon Islands.

1577–1580 English explorer Sir Francis Drake explores the Pacific during his round-the-world voyage.

1606 Dutch sailor Willem Jansz lands on the west coast of Australia.

1615 Luis Vaez de Torres of Spain explores coasts of New Guinea and northern Australia.

1642 Dutch sailor Abel Tasman explores the coast of Tasmania and New Zealand's South Island.

131

THE THIRTY YEARS WAR

The Thirty Years War began in 1618 as a protest by the Protestant noblemen of Bohemia (now part of the Czech Republic) against their Catholic rulers, the Habsburg Holy Roman emperors. The war ended in 1648 with the Treaty of Westphalia, which gave religious freedom and independence to Protestant states. The long war devastated many states in Germany. Some lost more than half their population through disease, famine, and fighting.

SWEDEN AT WAR
Gustavus II Adolphus of Sweden led his troops against the Habsburgs because he believed the Protestant religion was being destroyed.

King Gustavus II Adolphus always fought at the head of his men.

A RELIGIOUS WAR

In 1619 Ferdinand II became Holy Roman emperor but rebellion against his rule soon spread to Germany. In 1620 Ferdinand defeated the Protestant king Frederick and soon Catholicism was the only religion allowed in Bohemia. Spain, also ruled by the Habsburgs, joined the war on the side of the Holy Roman Empire. Believing the Protestant religion to be in danger, the Swedish king Gustavus II Adolphus joined the war against Spain and the Holy Roman Empire. France, although Catholic, also entered the war in order to curtail Habsburg power.

BOHEMIAN PROTEST
The Thirty Years War began after a group of Bohemians
threw two Catholics out of a castle window

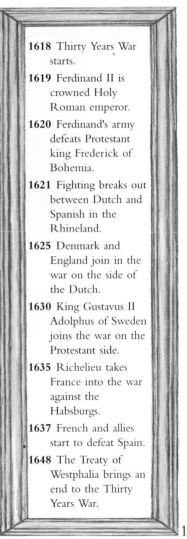

1618 Thirty Years War starts.

1619 Ferdinand II is crowned Holy Roman emperor.

1620 Ferdinand's army defeats Protestant king Frederick of Bohemia.

1621 Fighting breaks out between Dutch and Spanish in the Rhineland.

1625 Denmark and England join in the war on the side of the Dutch.

1630 King Gustavus II Adolphus of Sweden joins the war on the Protestant side.

1635 Richelieu takes France into the war against the Habsburgs.

1637 French and allies start to defeat Spain.

1648 The Treaty of Westphalia brings an end to the Thirty Years War.

THE DUTCH EMPIRE

In 1581 the northern provinces of the Netherlands, led by William of Orange, declared independence against Spanish rule. The newly independent Dutch started to build up a trading empire. In 1599 they took control of the Moluccas, or Spice Islands, from the Portuguese, and in 1602 the Dutch East India Company was founded to encourage more trade with the islands of the East Indies. Other Dutch merchants sailed westward and set up the Dutch West India Company, which traded in slaves, tobacco, and sugar.

Tea

Cinnamon

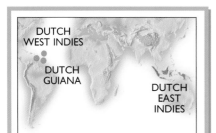

A TRADING EMPIRE
This map shows the Dutch trading empire. The Dutch East Indies (now Indonesia) were rich in spices. Sugar, rice, and slaves were traded in Guiana.

DUTCH WEST INDIES

DUTCH GUIANA

DUTCH EAST INDIES

COLONY IN AFRICA
The Dutch East India Company set up a colony at the Cape of Good Hope (southern Africa) to supply its ships sailing to the East Indies.

The Dutch traders bought goods from the locals.

Cloves

Coffee

WEALTH THROUGH TRADE

The highly successful trading empire helped to make the Dutch very wealthy people. Their chief city, Amsterdam, was home to many wealthy merchants and bankers. Trade was jealously guarded, and this led to wars with England in the late 1600s.

Fresh supplies were needed for the journey to the East Indies.

Dutch sailing ship

1568 Dutch led by William of Orange begin revolt against Spanish rule.

1581 The Republic of the United Netherlands declares independence. William of Orange is elected ruler.

1599 Dutch take control of the Moluccas from Portugal.

1602 Dutch East India Company is founded.

1621 Dutch West India Company is founded.

1648 Spain recognizes Dutch independence at the end of the Thirty Years War.

1651–1674 Three Anglo-Dutch wars between the Netherlands and England are fought over trade.

1689 William III of Orange and his wife Mary, daughter of James II of England, are offered the English throne. The Netherlands starts to decline as England becomes more powerful.

NORTH AMERICA

Many Native Americans helped early settlers to survive.

In the late sixteenth century, small groups of Europeans began to settle in North America. Sir Walter Raleigh made the first serious attempts at colonization in an area he called Virginia. These early colonies failed, but in 1607 Raleigh set up a more successful colony named Jamestown. Probably the most famous early settlers are the Pilgrim Fathers, a group of religious dissenters who left England in 1620 to practice their religion in peace. They founded a small settlement in Massachusetts. Early settlers relied heavily on help from, and trade with, the Native Americans to survive.

Sir Walter Raleigh

THE STRUGGLE TO COLONIZE

Early colonists, such as the explorer Sir Walter Raleigh, had to struggle against hunger, disease, and battles with the Native Americans, whose land they were occupying.

136

FRENCH EXPLORERS

French traders and missionaries set up colonies in the northern part of North America, which they called Canada. Samuel de Champlain founded Quebec in 1608. Later, French explorers in the south claimed the Mississippi River valley for France, calling it Louisiana after their king Louis XIV.

THE FIRST SETTLERS

The colonists earned their living by farming, producing food for themselves and crops for export to Europe. They built settlements near a good water supply.

The settlers cut down trees to build log cabin homes, and barns for their animals.

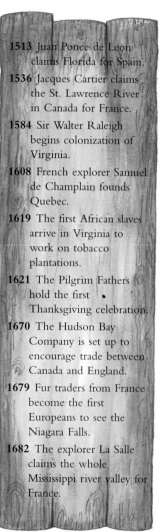

1513 Juan Ponce de Leon claims Florida for Spain.

1536 Jacques Cartier claims the St. Lawrence River in Canada for France.

1584 Sir Walter Raleigh begins colonization of Virginia.

1608 French explorer Samuel de Champlain founds Quebec.

1619 The first African slaves arrive in Virginia to work on tobacco plantations.

1621 The Pilgrim Fathers hold the first Thanksgiving celebration.

1670 The Hudson Bay Company is set up to encourage trade between Canada and England.

1679 Fur traders from France become the first Europeans to see the Niagara Falls.

1682 The explorer La Salle claims the whole Mississippi river valley for France.

Turkeys were kept for food.

ENGLISH CIVIL WAR

The English Civil War broke out during the reign of Charles I. The king came into regular conflict with parliament, which he dissolved in 1629. For 11 years Charles ruled without parliament's help, but he later recalled it in order to raise money to fight a rebellion in Scotland. When the king tried to arrest five of his opponents in parliament in 1642, civil war broke out. At first the king's forces, or Royalists, were more successful than Parliament's supporters, the Roundheads. Eventually, in 1645, the Roundheads defeated Charles's forces. Charles was found guilty of treason and executed in 1649.

A Roundhead soldier

MAJOR BATTLES
This map shows the main battles of the war. After 1644, the king's forces, the Royalists, held the pink areas. Parliament's soldiers, the Roundheads, controlled the green areas.

Preston X X Marston Moor
Adwalton Moor X ● YORK

X Naseby

Worcester X X Edgehill
Cropredy Bridge X
Bristol X OXFORD ● X Brentford
Roundway Down X X ● LONDON
Newbury

Lostwithiel
X ● PLYMOUTH

Plain woolen jacket

A Royalist soldier

Puritans were strict Protestants who dressed simply and disapproved of theater and dancing.

THE ENGLISH COMMONWEALTH

After Charles's death England became a commonwealth (republic) ruled by parliament. Later, Oliver Cromwell ruled as Lord Protector. His successor, his son Richard, was removed from office. In 1660 Charles I's son returned from exile to reign as Charles II.

DEATH OF THE KING

Charles I was found guilty of treason and executed in January 1649. The execution took place on a scaffold outside the banqueting hall of Whitehall.

Priest · Executioner · Charles I

1625 Charles I comes to the throne.

1629 Parliament tries to curb Charles's power and is dismissed.

1639 Rebellion breaks out in Scotland.

1641 Charles makes peace with the Scots, but rebellion breaks out in Ireland.

1642 Civil war begins. The first major battle takes place at Edgehill, Warwickshire.

1645 The New Model Army, led by Sir Thomas Fairfax and Oliver Cromwell, decisively defeats the Royalists.

1648 Charles starts a second civil war, but is quickly defeated.

1649 Charles is executed on January 31.

1653–1658 Oliver Cromwell rules as Lord Protector.

1660 Restoration of the monarchy; Charles II comes to the throne.

139

LOUIS XIV

Louis XIV of France was the most powerful European monarch in the seventeenth century. He became king in 1643 at the age of five, but his mother ruled on his behalf until 1651. There were constant arguments between her and the nobles who wanted a share of power. In 1661, Louis dismissed the council of nobles and ruled France on his own. His chief adviser was Jean Colbert, who reorganized taxes, reformed the legal system, and set up new industries. To protect France's position as Europe's dominant power, Colbert increased the size of the navy.

THE PALACE OF VERSAILLES
Louis's magnificent new palace was built on the site of a royal hunting lodge outside Paris.

THE PLAYS OF MOLIÈRE

One of the king's favorite dramatists was Jean Baptiste Molière (1622–1673). Molière wrote and directed many plays at Versailles, and he also acted in them.

FINANCIAL DISASTER

Louis spent vast sums of money on his palace at Versailles, and on three major wars between 1667 and 1697. When the Huguenots (Protestants) were persecuted by their Catholic rulers, around 300,000 of them, including skilled craft workers, fled abroad. The French economy suffered from their loss.

1638 Birth of Louis, son of Louis XIII of France and Anne of Austria.

1643 Louis XIV succeeds to the throne.

1661 Louis takes control of France.

1662 Work starts on rebuilding Versailles.

1667 Start of war with Spain over the Netherlands.

1672 Start of six-year Dutch war, which ends in victory for France.

1685 Persecution of the Huguenots. Many of them leave France.

1689–1697 War of the Grand Alliance, led by Britain, ends in French defeat.

1701–1713 War of the Spanish Succession. Louis wins the Spanish throne for his grandson, but brings France close to collapse.

1715 Louis XIV dies at the age of 77.

THE SLAVE TRADE

Africa had a long history of slavery, but the slave trade did not happen on a large scale until the early sixteenth century. At this time, European colonists in America and the Caribbean needed workers for their plantations. Europeans began visiting the coasts of Africa in search of slaves. Soon huge numbers of people were being captured, sold to European slave traders and taken across the Atlantic. During the eighteenth century, between six and seven million people were shipped to America. From the 1780s onward, some Europeans and Americans began to campaign against this trade.

Slaves wore heavy iron collars to make sure they could not rest while working.

THE SUGAR PLANTATIONS
For all the slaves on a plantation, the work was heavy, conditions were bad, and hours were long. Most were badly treated, underfed, and beaten.

ENGLAND
EUROPE
NORTH AMERICA
PORTUGAL
WEST INDIES
WEST AFRICA
BRAZIL

THE SLAVE ROUTE
Slave ships from Europe sailed on a triangular route. They sailed to Africa to buy the slaves, carried them to the Americas where the slaves were sold, and then returned home with sugar, rum, and cotton.

Some slaves worked in the fields, harvesting the sugarcane.

A LIFE OF SLAVERY

Slave ships carried more than 400 people, chained together and unable to move. Conditions were terrible, with not enough light, air, food, or water. Up to a third died on each 8-week journey. Slaves faced a hard life on the plantations, rarely surviving for more than 10 years.

Slaves also worked in the sugar factories.

1441 The first Portuguese ship brings slaves back from West Africa to Europe.

1448 Slaves are sold at the first Portuguese trading post set up in Africa.

1502 Spanish take the first slaves from Africa to America to work on plantations.

c. 1680 The average plantation in Barbados has 60 slaves.

1681 By now there are about 2,000 slaves in the American colony of Virginia.

1700s The slave trade is at its peak. Cities such as Bristol, Liverpool, and Nantes grow rich on the profits.

1730 By now, about 90 per cent of Jamaica's population are of African origin.

1780s People start to campaign against slavery.

REVOLUTION AND INDUSTRY

The world in turmoil 1700–1900

The two centuries between 1700 and 1900 were a time of conflict, revolution, and change in many parts of the world. Some of these changes were political, while others were economic or social. Empires were won and lost, kings and governments toppled, and agriculture, industry, and transportation developed. The countries of northwest Europe grew more powerful, while Spain and Portugal declined.

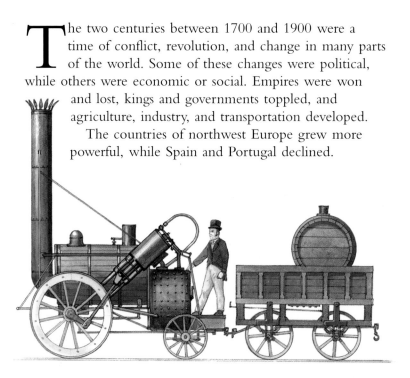

The 13 American colonies declared their independence from Britain in 1776 to become the United States of America. They were helped by the French, who in 1789 had their own revolution, overthrowing their king and becoming first a republic and then an empire.

Britain tightened its control on India throughout this period and laid claim to Australia and New Zealand and many islands in the Pacific. In the Scramble for Africa, between 1880 and 1900, the European powers divided up nearly the whole continent of Africa among themselves. China, Japan, and Russia stayed largely isolated.

THE RUSSIAN EMPIRE

Peter the Great transformed Russia from an isolated, backward nation into a major Europe power. He expanded the Russian navy and army, established a modern iron industry, and built new roads and canals. To reflect Russia's growing wealth and his own power, Peter moved the capital from Moscow to a new city, St. Petersburg.

PEASANT LIFE

In the countryside, life was a constant struggle for the Russian serfs (peasants). They paid heavy taxes and, if the harvest was bad, often faced starvation.

CATHERINE THE GREAT
Catherine was a ruthless and ambitious ruler, and many European leaders feared her power.

Wooden houses gave little protection from the bad weather.

146

PETER THE GREAT
Peter the Great was an immensely tall man—almost 7 feet (more than 2 m). His physical presence matched his energetic and strong-willed character. He could be brutal, even imprisoning and torturing his own son.

THE EMPRESS CATHERINE

Nearly 40 years after Peter's death, another powerful ruler, Catherine the Great, came to the throne. Catherine II (the Great) was Prussian by birth, but married the heir to the Russian throne. He was murdered after becoming czar and Catherine declared herself empress. Like Peter I, she encouraged western ideas and used warfare to gain territory for Russia, fighting the Ottoman Empire in 1774 and 1792, and Sweden in 1790. She also claimed much of Poland when it was partitioned (divided up).

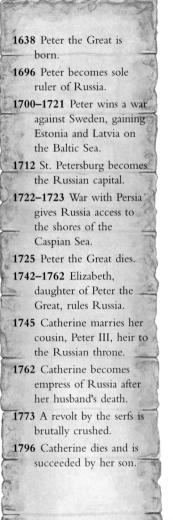

1638 Peter the Great is born.

1696 Peter becomes sole ruler of Russia.

1700–1721 Peter wins a war against Sweden, gaining Estonia and Latvia on the Baltic Sea.

1712 St. Petersburg becomes the Russian capital.

1722–1723 War with Persia gives Russia access to the shores of the Caspian Sea.

1725 Peter the Great dies.

1742–1762 Elizabeth, daughter of Peter the Great, rules Russia.

1745 Catherine marries her cousin, Peter III, heir to the Russian throne.

1762 Catherine becomes empress of Russia after her husband's death.

1773 A revolt by the serfs is brutally crushed.

1796 Catherine dies and is succeeded by her son.

MANCHU CHINA

In the early seventeenth century, the Chinese people rebelled against the high taxes imposed by the Ming Dynasty. In 1644, the Manchu tribes from northeast China seized power and set up a new dynasty, known as the Qing, which ruled China for more than 250 years. The Manchus considered themselves superior to the Chinese and lived apart from them. However, they followed the Chinese style of government and gradually they also adopted the Chinese way of life.

Emblem of five-clawed dragon

Embroidered gown of fine silk

THE CITY OF BEIJING
The Ming expanded Beijing greatly, adding many palaces and temples and building a new wall and moat around the city. The Qing left the inner city unaltered, but added new palaces and temples outside the city wall.

City walls

Much of China's wealth came from farming.

Silk trousers

A moat surrounded the inner city.

The Manchu wore their hair in a pigtail.

MANCHU STYLE
The emperor wore a silk gown embroidered with a five-clawed dragon. The Manchu wore superior clothes to the Chinese.

CHINESE EXPANSION

Under the Qing Dynasty, China's empire tripled in size, and the population grew from 150 million to 450 million. Production of silk, porcelain, lacquerware, and cotton expanded, and trade, especially with Europe, increased greatly. China produced almost all its own food. During the 18th century, it became increasingly difficult to restrict imports from Europe. The emperor, however, was determined to keep China isolated from outside influences.

RUSSIA
MONGOLIA · Beijing
KOREA
QING EMPIRE
INDIA
FORMOSA
ANNAM

_THE QING EMPIRE
The orange area on this map shows the extent of the Qing Dynasty's empire. It is much larger than China today, whose boundary is shown in blue._

1618 United Manchu tribes take control of the Chinese province of Liaotung.

1630s The Chinese people rebel against high taxes.

1644 The Manchus take control of Beijing and overthrow the Ming Dynasty.

1661 Kangxi becomes the second Qing emperor and opens up China to foreign trade and ideas.

1722 Death of Kangxi.

1736 Qianlong, grandson of Kangxi, becomes emperor and rules for 60 years.

1770 Qianlong's rule begins to decline as he tries to keep China isolated from the rest of the world.

1792 Lord Macartney, the first British ambassador to China, fails to obtain permission to increase trade.

1799 Qianlong dies.

1840 The Qing Dynasty starts to decline.

149

FARMING AND SCIENCE

Toward the end of the seventeenth century, more people began leaving the countryside to live in towns and cities. To provide enough food for everybody, better methods of farming were needed. Farmers in the Netherlands experimented with crop rotation, planting four different crops in the same field over a four-year period. This idea was copied in Belgium and Britain. Farm machinery, such as the plow, was improved, and the seed drill and hoe were invented. Land was reorganized into small fields separated by hedges or walls. Farmers experimented with breeding bigger cattle, sheep, and pigs.

VOLUMES OF KNOWLEDGE
The French Encyclopédie *was written by experts in many different subjects. It comprised 17 text volumes and 11 volumes of pictures.*

A worker rakes over the holes.

NEW MACHINES
A seed drill made a series of even holes into which seeds fell. Before the drill was invented, seeds were scattered by hand.

Heavy horses pull the equipment.

The seed drill makes a row of holes.

150

FANTAIL WINDMILLS
The fantail windmill was invented in 1745. The fantail moved the main sails whenever the wind changed. The sails of earlier windmills had to be repositioned continuously.

NEW IDEAS

The Enlightenment was a period when new ideas about government, personal freedom and religious beliefs developed in Europe. Philosophers and writers looked at the role of people within the whole world. They challenged the idea of absolute monarchy and the traditional privileges of the nobility and clergy.

Ballet was performed in public for the first time during the eighteenth century. Ballerinas wore clothes that were less constricting.

1687 Sir Isaac Newton publishes his theories about light, the laws of motion, and gravity.

1701 Jethro Tull invents the seed drill.

1730 Introduction in England of four-crop rotation.

1759–1801 British parliament passes acts to enclose more than 7,000,000 acres of common land.

1743 Benjamin Franklin sets up the American Philosophical Society in Philadelphia.

1751 The first volume of the *Encyclopédie* is published.

1768 The *Encyclopaedia Britannica* is first published.

1788 *The Times* newspaper is first published.

1792 Mary Wollstonecraft's *A Vindication of the Rights of Women* argues for equal opportunities in education for everyone.

AUSTRIA AND PRUSSIA

Europe in the eighteenth century was dominated by absolute monarchs whose "enlightened" courts attracted artists and intellectuals. Two of the richest and most powerful states were Austria and Prussia. Austria was ruled by the Habsburgs, but the lands under their control had become so large that the emperor, Charles V, divided them. One half was governed from Madrid in Spain, the other from Vienna in Austria. In 1740 Maria Theresa came to the Austrian throne. She pulled Austria back from virtual bankruptcy, and under her rule Austria became the artistic center of Europe.

THE SCHONBRUNN
PALACE
The Habsburgs' summer palace in Vienna was intended to rival the palace of Versailles. It had 1,440 rooms set in formal gardens.

THE AUSTRIAN COURT
Musicians such as Wolfgang Amadeus Mozart (1756–1791) played at the court of Maria Theresa. Under her rule, Austria became the artistic center of Europe.

Mozart had first played at court when he was only six years old.

SEVEN YEARS WAR
The Seven Years War (1756–1763) was a clash of interests between European powers. France, Austria, and Russia opposed Prussia and Britain.

FREDERICK THE GREAT

Frederick II (the Great) became king of Prussia in 1740. He was an outstanding general, his greatest victory being at Rossbach (1757) when he routed a combined French and Austrian army twice the size of his own. Under Frederick's leadership, Prussia emerged as a major European power. He introduced economic reforms and religious freedom, and abolished torture.

1700 The last Spanish Habsburg monarch dies.

1701 Frederick I becomes king of Prussia.

1711 Charles VI, Archduke of Austria, becomes Holy Roman emperor.

1713 Frederick William succeeds as king of Prussia. He centralizes government and creates a powerful regular army.

1740 Maria Theresa, daughter of Charles VI, inherits the Austrian throne. Frederick II (the Great) becomes king of Prussia.

1756–1763 Seven Years War. France, Austria, and Russia clash with Britain and Prussia.

1757 Prussia defeats a much larger Austrian and French army at the battle of Rossbach.

1781 Joseph, Maria Theresa's son and successor, introduces major reforms and frees the serfs.

1786 Frederick the Great dies.

BIRTH OF THE USA

Fighting between British and French colonists in North America ended in 1763 when the British gained control of Canada with the signing of the Treaty of Paris. By 1770 the British colonists were increasingly unhappy with the British government. Although they paid British taxes they had no say in how government was run. In June 1775, the colonists' army, under George Washington, clashed with British troops at Bunker Hill, outside Boston. The British won, but the War of Independence had begun.

GEORGE WASHINGTON
On Christmas night 1776, George Washington led his troops across the ice-strewn Delaware River and went on to defeat the British at the battle of Trenton. In 1789, he was elected the first president of the United States.

George Washington was commander of the American forces.

154

PAUL REVERE

Paul Revere, a hero of the Revolutionary War, rode from Boston to Lexington to warn of the approaching British soldiers. Although he was captured, his mission was successful.

THE REVOLUTIONARY WAR

Flintlock musket

Long-tailed coat

On July 4, 1776 the colonial leaders passed the Declaration of Independence, which the British government refused to accept. With improved equipment and training, the colonists' army began defeating the British. The war ended in 1781 when the British surrendered. In 1783, Britain recognized an independent United States of America.

British infantrymen wore red long-tailed coats and so were known as "redcoats." Trained for fighting in European wars, they found fighting in America very different.

1763 End of the Seven Years War. Britain gains control of French territory in Canada.

1765 Protests start against British taxes in the American colonies.

1773 At the Boston Tea Party, colonists throw ships' cargoes overboard to protest against the tax on tea.

1775 The American War of Independence starts.

1776 On July 4 the Declaration of Independence is adopted.

1777 France joins war on America's side.

1777 British capture Philadelphia, in Pennsylvania.

1779 Spain joins the war on America's side.

1780 The Dutch join war on America's side.

1781 After a siege at Yorktown, Virginia, the British Army surrenders.

155

FRENCH REVOLUTION

 In the eighteenth century, French society was divided into three estates, or classes: the nobility, the clergy and the third estate was the common people. Only the third estate paid taxes. In 1788, poorer people faced starvation after a bad harvest. When the king, Louis XVI, tried to raise more money for the government, the third estate rebelled. The Bastille royal prison was attacked, and riots broke out across France. The Revolution had begun.

THE GUILLOTINE
During the Reign of Terror around 500,000 people were arrested, and 17,000 of them were put to death by public execution on the guillotine.

Guillotine

Executioner

Large crowds gathered to watch the executions.

Many of the victims were aristocrats.

156

THE REIGN OF TERROR

In August 1789, the Declaration of the Rights of Man was made. Louis XVI was arrested, and his execution in 1793 marked the start of the Reign of Terror led by Maximilien Robespierre. Over nine months thousands of opponents of the Revolution were executed. Austria, Britain, the Netherlands, Prussia, and Spain declared war on France. Frightened by events, Robespierre's colleagues ordered his execution.

MAXIMILIEN
ROBESPIERRE (1758–1794)
Robespierre was a lawyer who
was elected to the Estates
General in 1789. In 1793, he
started the Reign of Terror. He
himself was later denounced and
guillotined, and his execution
ended the Reign of Terror.

1789 The third estate forms the National Assembly. On July 14, the French Revolution starts when a mob seizes the Bastille. On August 26 the Declaration of the Rights of Man is made. On October 5 a mob fetches the king and his family back to Paris as prisoners.

1792 France is declared a republic.

1793 Louis XVI and Marie Antoinette are executed. The Reign of Terror starts. Austria, Britain, the Netherlands, Prussia, and Spain are at war with France.

1794 Robespierre is executed. France is governed by the *Directoire,* a committee of five men.

1795 Napoleon Bonaparte defends Paris against rebels.

OCEANIA

The first European to see the continent of Australia was the Dutchman Willem Janzoon, who landed on the northeast coast in about 1605. Another Dutchman, Abel Tasman, sailed from Batavia (Indonesia) in 1642 and visited Tasmania, New Zealand, Tonga, and Fiji. Between 1768 and 1779, the British navigator, James Cook, made three voyages to the Pacific. On his first voyage, aboard the *Endeavour,* he took scientists and artists to record the plants, animals and people they met. They sailed around New Zealand, then to Australia. Cook landed at Botany Bay and claimed the territory for Britain, even though Aboriginal Australians already lived there.

ABORIGINAL ART
Aboriginal paintings on rocks and tree bark often depicted animals and people, in very stylized forms.

EXPLORER ROUTES
This map shows the voyages of Willem Janzoon, Abel Tasman, and James Cook. These three men did more than any other Europeans to map the coasts of the Pacific Ocean.

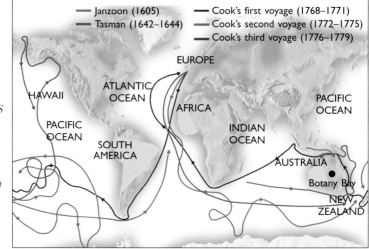

— Janzoon (1605)
— Tasman (1642–1644)
— Cook's first voyage (1768–1771)
— Cook's second voyage (1772–1775)
— Cook's third voyage (1776–1779)

EUROPE
HAWAII
ATLANTIC OCEAN
AFRICA
PACIFIC OCEAN
PACIFIC OCEAN
SOUTH AMERICA
INDIAN OCEAN
AUSTRALIA
Botany Bay
NEW ZEALAND

COOK VISITS NEW ZEALAND

Captain James Cook and his crew met Maoris in New Zealand for the first time in 1769. He attempted to establish good relations with the New Zealand people.

Cook's ship, the Endeavour

Maori chief

Cook spent six months charting the New Zealand coast.

CONVICTS AND SETTLERS

In 1788 the British government started transporting convicts to the penal colony of Port Jackson, in Australia. From 1793, increasing numbers of free settlers joined the convicts. The settlers had little respect for the Aboriginal Australians whose homelands they were stealing. Settlers in New Zealand treated the Maoris in the same way.

1605 Willem Janzoon lands in Australia but does not venture inland.

1642 Abel Tasman explores the South Pacific.

1644 Tasman sails along Australia's north coast.

1768–1771 Captain James Cook's first voyage to the South Pacific.

1772–1775 Cook's second voyage.

1776 Cook's third voyage. It ends in 1779 when Cook is killed in Hawaii.

1788 British convicts are transported to Australia's first penal colony.

1793 The first free settlers from Britain settle around Botany Bay.

1840 The Treaty of Waitangi grants land rights and British citizenship to the Maoris. The treaty is not honored and war breaks out (1843–1848).

1851 The Gold Rush brings more settlers to Australia.

NAPOLEON

Napoleon Bonaparte made his name in the French army, rising to become the Emperor of France. He became an officer at the age of 16, and won his first victory against rebels during the French Revolution. In 1798 the French army, under Napoleon, defeated the Egyptians and the Ottomans, but the French navy was itself defeated by the British at the battle of the Nile. Napoleon overthrew the *Directoire*, or committee, that ruled France and in 1804 he proclaimed himself Emperor.

THE CODE NAPOLEON
Napoleon introduced a code of laws that incorporated many of the ideas of the French Revolution.

THE BATTLE OF AUSTERLITZ
In December 1805, a French army of 73,000, under the command of Napoleon and his generals, defeated an army of 87,000 Austrians and Russians. The enemy was lured into a valley where many were killed.

This map shows the French empire under Napoleon I and the dependent states that were virtually part of it. The main battles of the Napoleonic Wars are also shown

The empire
Dependent states
X Battles

Borodino X
X Friedland
Smolensk
Waterloo X   X Leipzig
Lutzen X
X Jena   X Austerlitz
Hohenlinden X   X Wagram
Vittoria
X   Marengo X
X Torres Vedras
X Trafalgar

THE NAPOLEONIC WARS

Napoleon was a brilliant general who commanded thousands of conscripted men. In 1805 the British, under Lord Nelson, defeated the French fleet at Trafalgar. On land, Napoleon seemed undefeatable, but in 1812 his invasion of Russia was disastrous and his army in Spain suffered setbacks. After abdicating in 1814, he raised a new army the following year. Napoleon was defeated at the battle of Waterloo.

1769 Birth of Napoleon at Ajaccio, Corsica.

1795 Napoleon defends Paris against rebels.

1798 Nelson defeats the French fleet at the battle of the Nile, Egypt.

1802 Napoleon plans to invade Britain.

1803 Britain declares war on France.

1804 Napoleon declares himself emperor of France.

1805 Nelson defeats French fleet at Trafalgar. Napoleon defeats the Austrians and Russians at the battle of Austerlitz.

1812 Napoleon's army invades Russia but is defeated by the harsh climate.

1814 Napoleon is forced to abdicate and is exiled.

1815 Napoleon raises a new army. He is defeated at the battle of Waterloo.

1821 Napoleon dies in exile.

161

SOUTH AMERICA

In the early nineteenth century Spain and Portugal still ruled vast colonies in South America, but the colonists had begun to fight for their independence. The main struggle against Spanish rule was led by Simón Bolívar from Venezuela and José de San Martin from Argentina. San Martin gained freedom for his country in 1816, but Bolívar's fight was longer and more difficult. He joined a rebel army that captured Caracas, capital of Venezuela, in 1810, but was defeated by the Spanish. Bolívar became the army's leader but was defeated by the Spanish again.

THE BATTLE OF AYACHUCHO
At the battle of Ayachucho in 1824, Simón Bolívar's army defeated the Spanish. He had finally secured independence for Peru. Part of the newly liberated Peru became the republic of Bolívia, named for Bolívar.

JOSÉ DE SAN MARTIN

José de San Martin freed Argentina from Spanish rule. He then led his army over the Andes mountains to help the Chilean people gain their independence.

FREEDOM FROM SPANISH RULE

In 1819, Bolívar led his army over the Andes into Colombia and defeated the Spanish in a surprise attack. He later freed Venezuela, Ecuador, and Panama from Spanish rule, making them part of the Republic of Gran Colombia. Bolívar became president of the new state.

BOLIVIANS TODAY
Today, Bolivians wear dress that combines ancient patterns with Spanish influences.

1808 Independence struggles begin in South America.

1816 José de San Martin leads Argentina to independence from Spain.

1817 At the battle of Chacabuco in Chile, San Martin and Bernado O'Higgins are victorious over the Spanish.

1818 Chile becomes independent from Spain.

1819 Simón Bolívar defeats the Spanish at the battle of Boyoca. Colombia wins independence from Spain.

1821 Bolívar's victory over the Spanish at Carabobo ensures independence for Venezuela.

1822 Brazil wins independence from Portugal.

1824 Bolívar wins independence for Peru.

1825 Bolivia is named for Bolívar.

1828 Uruguay wins independence from Spain.

163

INDUSTRIAL REVOLUTION

The Industrial Revolution transformed Britain as people moved to the towns to work in factories. New inventions and discoveries made the revolution possible.

Abraham Darby discovered that iron could be smelted with coke, and Thomas Newcomen improved the steam engine. Until the 1760s woolen or linen cloth was produced by hand. The invention of the flying shuttle and Hargreaves' Spinning Jenny speeded up the weaving process and increased yarn production. Factories were built to house the machinery and a large-scale cotton industry began to develop.

THE FIRST PASSENGER RAILROAD
The first public railroad, from Stockton to Darlington in England, opened in 1825. From 1830, steam locomotives were used to draw covered passenger carriages.

Children worked in coal mines from the age of five. They pulled heavy loads or sat all day in total darkness opening and closing doors to let the air circulate.

Passenger carriages

A separate truck carried coal and water for the boiler.

Spindles of cotton

SPINNING JENNY

In 1764, James Hargreaves invented the Spinning Jenny, which allowed one person to spin eight threads at once. He named his new machine after his daughter, Jenny.

The machine was operated by a large wheel.

Steam locomotive

FROM COAL MINES TO CANALS

The use of steam power increased the demand for coal, and also for iron to make steam engines and other machinery. Coal mines became bigger and deeper and iron works expanded. Canals and railroads were built to bring raw materials to the factories and take finished goods away.

1709 Darby discovers smelting iron with coke.

1712 Newcomen develops improved steam engine to pump water out of mines.

1733 Kay invents the flying shuttle.

1742 First cotton factories set up in Birmingham and Northampton.

1759 Bridgewater Canal is built to carry coal from the mines.

1764 Hargreaves invents the Spinning Jenny.

1769 Watt designs a more efficient steam engine. Arkwright invents a spinning frame powered by water.

1779 First iron bridge is built.

1808 Trevithick demonstrates his steam locomotive in London.

1815 Davy's safety lamp warns miners of explosive gas.

1825 The first passenger railroad from Stockton to Darlington opens.

165

EUROPE IN TURMOIL

In the mid-nineteenth century, much of Europe was in chaos. The population had almost doubled in 100 years, and many people were poor. There was not enough spare land in the countryside, while in the towns jobs were in short supply. Ordinary people wanted a say in government and a share in their country's wealth. Revolt broke out in France in 1830 and quickly spread to other countries.

Riots broke out in Berlin in 1848.

Prussian soldiers crushed the riots.

Women and children were brutally attacked.

THE YEAR OF REVOLUTIONS

In 1848 revolutions and protests broke out again throughout Europe. In Britain, the Chartists demonstrated for political reforms and votes for all men. In Ireland, people agitated for an independent republic. French rioters demanded votes for all men and a new republic. In Germany, and also in Italy, people wanted the separate self-governing states to

- ● Centers of revolution in 1848

Berlin · PRUSSIA
Frankfurt ●
● Paris ● Warsaw
FRANCE ● Prague
AUSTRIAN ● Vienna
EMPIRE ● Budapest
Milan ●
Venice
● Rome

The map shows the main centers of unrest in 1848.

unite into one country. All these revolutions were squashed by the end of 1849, but the ideas that drove them remained.

UNREST IN SICILY
The revolutions of 1848 were sparked off by a small revolt in Palermo, in Sicily. Soon the spirit of protest had spread across Europe.

1830 Riots break out as ordinary people demand a say in government.

1831 Belgium declares independence from the Netherlands.

1832 Greece becomes independent from the Ottoman Empire.

1838 In Britain, the People's Charter is published to demand political reforms. Its supporters become known as Chartists.

1841–1848 Chartist campaign for votes for all men is led by an Irishman, Feargus O'Connor.

1844 Friedrich Engels makes a study of the lives of workers in Manchester, England.

1848 The Year of Revolutions affects most of Europe. The German socialists Karl Marx and Friedrich Engels publish their ideas as "The Communist Manifesto."

1852 In France, the Second Republic is replaced by the Second Empire.

EXPLORING AFRICA

Europeans hardly ever ventured beyond the coastal trading posts in Africa, but people gradually became more curious about the continent's interior. Many Europeans, including large numbers of missionaries, were sent out to Africa. The largest European settlement was Cape Colony in southern Africa. Most of the colonists were Dutch farmers, called Boers, but by 1835 they were unhappy under British rule. The Boers embarked on the Great Trek into the interior, but they came into conflict with the Zulus.

THE GREAT TREK
On the Great Trek the Boers went north from the Cape Colony in search of new lands. Trekkers tried to settle in Natal but were defeated by the Zulus.

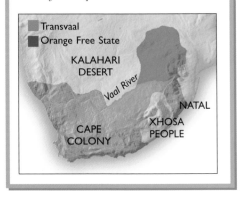

British soldier

Zulu warrior

Round-headed club, or knobkerry

ZULU WARFARE
Warfare was an important part of Zulu life, and from the 1820s they were the most powerful state in southern Africa.

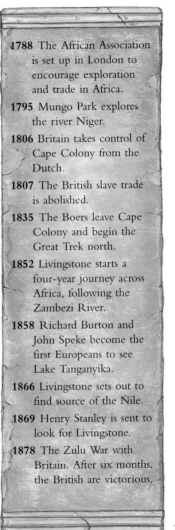

Henry Stanley   _David Livingstone_

STANLEY MEETS LIVINGSTONE
Henry Stanley found David Livingstone encamped at Ujiji on the shores of Lake Tanganyika in 1871. They spent several months exploring together, before Stanley returned to England.

BRITISH EXPEDITIONS

Many British expeditions explored Africa's interior between 1768 and 1875. From 1852 to 1856 David Livingstone crossed Africa following the Zambezi River. Later, he set out to look for the source of the Nile. The journalist Henry Stanley's expedition of 1879 along the Congo River was paid for by the Belgian king, who wanted to establish an overseas empire.

1788 The African Association is set up in London to encourage exploration and trade in Africa.

1795 Mungo Park explores the river Niger.

1806 Britain takes control of Cape Colony from the Dutch.

1807 The British slave trade is abolished.

1835 The Boers leave Cape Colony and begin the Great Trek north.

1852 Livingstone starts a four-year journey across Africa, following the Zambezi River.

1858 Richard Burton and John Speke become the first Europeans to see Lake Tanganyika.

1866 Livingstone sets out to find source of the Nile.

1869 Henry Stanley is sent to look for Livingstone.

1878 The Zulu War with Britain. After six months, the British are victorious.

169

EUROPEANS IN ASIA

By the seventeenth century, European trade with Asia was so important that the British, Dutch, and French each set up East India Companies to protect it. The Dutch concentrated on Indonesia, and by 1763 the British East India Company controlled India. In the 1830s, the Dutch decided they wanted to oversee agriculture on the Indonesian islands. They set up plantations to grow crops, such as coffee, for cash. This made enormous profits for Indonesian princes and Dutch colonists. However, ordinary people no longer had the time or the land to grow the crops they needed.

THE BRITISH IN INDIA
Many Europeans in India tried to live exactly as they would have done at home. Here Lady Impey, wife of the British Chief Justice of Bengal, is supervising Indian tailors. Although in India, her surroundings are typically British.

BRITISH CONTROL
This map shows the extent of British-controlled territory in India from 1757. The dependent states were ruled by Indian princes under British protection. Until 1947, India also included the countries of Pakistan and Bangladesh.

British-style furniture

Indian tailors at work

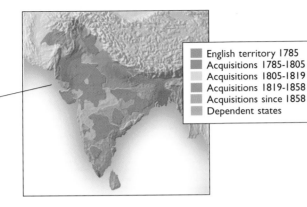

English territory 1785
Acquisitions 1785-1805
Acquisitions 1805-1819
Acquisitions 1819-1858
Acquisitions since 1858
Dependent states

COLONIES IN SOUTHEAST ASIA

One of the earliest British colonies in Southeast Asia was Singapore. By 1896 the British controlled Malaya, ruling through the local sultans. In the 1850s France began to take control of Indochina (now Cambodia and Vietnam). Although local people resisted French colonization, they were eventually defeated.

A LIFE OF LUXURY
Officials of the East India Company were usually very wealthy and enjoyed a luxurious lifestyle. They had many servants, and were often carried in enclosed litters, called palanquins.

1763 British East India Company takes control of India.

1786 The British take control of Penang in Malaysia.

1789 The French East India Company ceases to exist.

1819 British colony of Singapore is founded.

1824–1885 The Anglo-Burmese wars when Britain tries to take control of Burma.

1842 China cedes Hong Kong to Britain.

1856 Indian mutiny leads to British government taking control of India from the East India Company.

1884 French victory at the battle of Bac-Ninh in Indochina.

1885 Britain finally defeats the Burmese, making Burma part of India.

1887 French form Indochina, from Cambodia and Cochinchina, Tonkin, and Annam (Vietnam).

171

THE BRITISH EMPIRE

When Queen Victoria succeeded to the throne in 1837 Britain was one of the world's richest and most powerful countries. It was also a land of great contrasts, with landowners and industrialists living in luxury, while the poor led very hard lives. Much of Britain's wealth came from her colonies, which were eventually known as the British Empire. They mainly provided raw materials for British factories and a ready market for their goods. At its greatest extent, the Empire contained a quarter of the world's land and a quarter of its people.

QUEEN VICTORIA
Queen Victoria (1819–1901) came to the throne at the age of 18 and reigned for almost 64 years. After the death of her husband, Prince Albert in 1861, she remained in deep mourning for many years.

UNITED
KINGDOM

EGYPT

INDIA

SUDAN

NIGERIA

SOUTH
AFRICA

COMMONWEALTH
OF AUSTRALIA

■ British Empire

■ British protectorates

A GLOBAL EMPIRE
This map shows the British Empire in 1821. It was the largest empire the world had ever seen.

A TIME OF CHANGE

Under British rule, the economies of many colonies changed as plantations were created to produce tea, sugar, coffee, and spices for the British market. Other plantations produced rubber or cotton. Many British people emigrated to Canada, Australia, and New Zealand, where they set up cattle and sheep farms.

FLORENCE NIGHTINGALE
Florence Nightingale worked in military hospitals during the Crimean War, in which Russia fought against Turkey, France, and Britain.

1763 Britain takes control of Canada.

1808 Sierra Leone becomes a British colony.

1815 Treaty of Vienna gives Cape Colony (South Africa), Ceylon (Sri Lanka), Mauritius, and Malta to Britain.

1829 Britain claims the whole of Australia.

1837–1901 Reign of Queen Victoria.

1840 By the Treaty of Waitangi Britain takes New Zealand.

1843 The Gambia becomes a British colony.

1851 The Great Exhibition in London displays Britain's industrial and trading success.

1853–1856 The Crimean War.

1860 Lagos (Nigeria) is added to the Empire.

1867 Canada becomes a British Dominion.

1876 Victoria is crowned empress of India.

173

THE AMERICAN WEST

The first settlers from Europe made their homes in the eastern states. In 1803, the area west of the Mississippi was sold to the US. Explorers and traders began to venture farther west, setting up trails that the settlers later followed. People known as pioneers started making the long journey westward in trains of covered wagons. They took everything they needed to set up their new homes.

BEAST OF THE PLAINS
Bison (or buffalo) lived on the Great Plains. Native Americans depended on the bison for food, shelter, and clothing.

THE LONG JOURNEY

Long trains of covered wagons took pioneers westward. Inside was food, clothing, tools, and furniture. Water was stored in a barrel slung on the side. Wagons were often attacked by Native Americans whose land was being taken.

The wagons had massive wheels and strong axles.

Covered wagon

Water barrel

PIONEER LIFE

Each pioneer family cleared an area of land for farming. Timber from the trees they chopped was used to build homes. If crops failed, families would go hungry or gather food from the wild. In 1862, each family who would settle for at least five years received land from the government, in exchange for a small fee. Thousands took up the offer, and soon towns and cities began to spring up everywhere.

THE GOLD RUSH
The discovery of gold in California in 1848 attracted thousands of prospectors. They washed the river gravel in large pans, hoping to find gold.

A team of oxen or mules pulled each wagon.

1803 United States buys the lands west of the Mississippi from France.

1821 Opening of the Santa Fe Trail from Missouri to New Mexico.

1845 Europeans emigrate to the US, especially from Ireland and Germany.

1846 War breaks out between the United States and Mexico over land boundaries.

1848 The Guadalupe-Hidalgo Treaty ends the Mexican–American War.

1849 Height of the Gold Rush.

1859 Many new mines open in Nevada and Colorado.

1862 The Homestead Act encourages farmers to move to the Great Plains.

1867 United States buys Alaska from Russia.

1869 The Union Pacific Railroad is completed.

1882 Huge copper deposits are discovered at Butte, Montana.

175

AMERICAN CIVIL WAR

In the United States, by the early nineteenth century, industry and trade had developed in the North. In the South, agriculture and slavery dominated. When Abraham Lincoln, who opposed slavery, was elected president, 11 southern states formed their own Confederacy. This marked the beginning of the Civil War.

ULYSSES S. GRANT
Grant commanded the Union armies and led them to victory.

THE BATTLE OF BULL RUN

The battle of Bull Run, Virginia, in 1861 was the first major battle of the Civil War. Confederate forces defeated the Union army.

Union soldiers wore blue uniforms.

Cannon mounted on wheels.

Confederate forces wore gray uniforms.

GENERAL ROBERT E. LEE
Although Lee's Confederate forces were defeated, he was an outstanding leader.

NORTH VERSUS SOUTH

The North had more soldiers and more money, and the industry to provide weapons. It controlled the navy and was able to blockade southern ports, preventing the South from exporting cotton and getting supplies from abroad. The South won the early battles of the war, but in 1863, the war turned in the North's favor when Unionist troops defeated Confederate forces at Gettysburg, Pennsylvania. Lincoln announced his aim to abolish slavery throughout the United States. By the time the Confederates surrendered in 1865, much of the South lay in ruins.

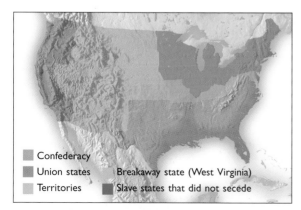

- Confederacy
- Union states
- Territories
- Breakaway state (West Virginia)
- Slave states that did not secede

1861 Civil War starts when Confederate troops attack the Union garrison at Fort Sumter, South Carolina. Confederates win the battle of Bull Run, Virginia.

1862 Confederate general Lee prevents Union army taking Richmond, Virginia and defeats another Union army at Fredericksburg, Virginia.

1863 Emancipation Proclamation is signed. Lee is defeated at Gettysburg, Pennsylvania. Grant's Union army captures Vicksburg, Mississippi.

1864 Union forces besiege Confederates at Petersburg, Virginia.

1865 Grant's forces capture Richmond, Virginia. On April 9, Lee surrenders to Grant, bringing the war to an end. On April 15, President Lincoln is assassinated by Confederate sympathizer John Wilkes Booth.

NATIVE AMERICANS

Many different tribes of Native Americans lived in North America, each with its own language and way of life. On the west coast, Native Americans fished for food, while in the east they grew corn and trapped animals. The arrival of European settlers was disastrous for Native Americans. They had no resistance to measles and smallpox, which the Europeans introduced. Many were also killed in land disputes.

In 1830 the government forced Native Americans in the east to live on distant reservations, while their lands were given to settlers.

GERONIMO
Geronimo was an Apache chief who became a fierce warrior after Mexican troops killed his family.

EXPERT WARRIORS
Native Americans fought a series of wars to keep their land and prevent starvation. Their battle tactics often terrified the enemy.

Framework of wooden poles

The Sioux were the largest tribe of the Great Plains. They lived in tepees, which could be quickly put up or taken down and were easy to transport. They were ideal for hunters following buffalo across the plains.

TRIBAL RESISTANCE

Throughout the century Europeans claimed still more land to the west. Native American resistance was put down harshly, although the Sioux defeated the US Army at the battle of the Little Bighorn in 1876. In 1890, over 200 unarmed Sioux were massacred at Wounded Knee Creek.

Hand-painted designs

Buffalo hide

Carved stone pipe

1830 The Indian Removal Act forces all Native Americans to move to reservations.

1838 Thousands of Cherokees die on the "Trail of Tears" march to the west.

1861–1890 Frequent wars break out between settlers and Native Americans.

1862 The Homestead Act allows settlers to buy land very cheaply.

1865 Many more settlers head west after the Civil War.

1876 Sioux and Cheyenne warriors trap and kill General Custer's forces at the battle of the Little Bighorn.

1890 The US cavalry massacres more than 200 Sioux at Wounded Knee.

1952 Reservations are abolished—Native Americans are free to live where they want.

179

ITALY AND GERMANY

When Napoleon was defeated in 1815, Italy and Germany were made up of many different states. Italy's states were given back to their foreign rulers, only Piedmont–Sardinia remaining independent. Opposition to foreign rule grew, and people campaigned for an independent and united Italy. Revolutions broke out in many states in 1848, but were crushed. In 1860 Giuseppe Garibaldi led a successful revolt, conquering Sicily and Naples. The northern states and Piedmont-Sardinia accepted Victor Emmanuel II as king, and in 1860 Garibaldi handed Naples and Sicily to him. Italy became a kingdom in 1861.

UNIFICATION ACROSS EUROPE
The top map shows the independent German states before unification. For centuries, these states formed the core of the Holy Roman Empire. The bottom map shows the unification of the Italian states over a 10-year period. The area around Rome was the last to join.

The Holy Roman Empire
Extent of the German Confederation

LOMBARDY
VENETIA
PIEDMONT
● Venice
PARMA
MODENA
LUCCA   ROMAGNA
TUSCANY
PAPAL STATES

Piedmont–Sardinia
Area added 1860
Area added 1866
Area added 1870

Rome ★

Adriatic Sea

Naples ●

SARDINIA

KINGDOM OF
THE TWO SICILIES

SICILY   Mediterranean
Sea

A UNITED GERMANY

In 1815, 38 states formed the German Confederation. In 1866, war between Austria and Prussia, the two most powerful states, ended in Prussian victory. France's emperor, Napoleon III, declared war on Prussia in 1870. Prussia won, and the German Second Empire was created under Prussian rule.

OTTO VON BISMARCK
Bismarck (1815–1898) became Prussian foreign minister in 1862. When Germany was united in 1871, Bismarck became its first chancellor.

Garibaldi — — Victor Emmanuel

UNIFICATION OF ITALY
Garibaldi handed the Kingdom of the Two Sicilies to Victor Emmanuel in 1860. Victor Emmanuel was proclaimed king of a united Italy the following year.

1815 After being briefly united under Napoleon I, the Italian states are divided up. Thirty-eight German states form the German Confederation.

1848 Unsuccessful revolutions break out in many Italian and German states to bring about unification.

1849 Victor Emmanuel II becomes king of Piedmont–Sardinia.

1860 Garibaldi and his Redshirts conquer the Kingdom of the Two Sicilies.

1861 Victor Emmanuel II becomes king of a unified Italy.

1866 Prussia wins the Seven Weeks War against Austria. The North German Confederation is set up.

1870–1871 Franco-Prussian War is won by Prussia.

1871 Creation of the German Second Empire, ruled by William II, former king of Prussia.

AFRICA DIVIDED

In 1880 less than five percent of Africa was ruled by European powers. Within 20 years seven European nations had control of virtually the whole continent, in what became known as the Scramble for Africa. The Europeans were helped by the opening of the Suez Canal, shortening the journey to Africa's east coast. They were also helped by the arrival of steamships and by medicines enabling them to survive disease. By 1884 Belgium, Britain, France, Portugal, and Spain had claimed new colonies or expanded old ones. Germany and Italy wanted their share of Africa too.

THE SCRAMBLE FOR AFRICA
This map shows Africa in 1914, when the European powers had finished establishing colonies there. Seven nations took control of the whole of Africa. Only two countries on the continent remained independent: Ethiopia and Liberia.

Morocco
Rio de Oro
Algeria
Libya
Sahara
Egypt
Gambia
French West Africa
Anglo Egyptian Sudan
Italian Somaliland
Ivory Coast
Nigeria
Ethiopia
Sierra Leone
Togoland
Belgian Congo
British East Africa
Gold Coast
German East Africa
Camerouns
Angola
Portugues East Afric
German Southwest Africa
Madagascar
Union of South Africa

■ British		■ Portuguese	
■ French		■ Belgian	
■ German		■ Spanish	
■ Italian			

EUROPEAN CONTROL

In 1884, the European powers divided Africa among themselves with no regard for African peoples or any natural boundaries. Any African resistance was crushed by large and well-equipped armies from Europe, and many thousands died fighting. Others suffered hardship and hunger as they were forced to work as cheap labor in mines and on crop plantations.

CECIL RHODES
Rhodes became prime minister of the Cape Colony. He helped to bring more territory under British control.

THE BOER STRUGGLE
During the 1830s many Boers had left Cape Colony and headed north to escape British rule. Britain and the Boer people fought the Boer Wars (1899–1902) for control of southern Africa. African peoples, caught in the struggle between these two groups of whites, suffered greatly.

1882 Britain takes control of Egypt to secure access to the Suez Canal.

1884 The Conference of Berlin divides Africa up among seven European countries.

1889 The British conquer the land of the Matabele, calling it Rhodesia.

1891 Tanganyika (now Tanzania) becomes a German protectorate. Northern Algeria becomes part of France.

1893 The French take control of Mali.

1895 Kenya comes under British control.

1899–1902 The Boer Wars between Britain and the Boer people.

1910 The Union of South Africa is formed.

1911 The British colony of Rhodesia is divided into Northern Rhodesia (now Zambia) and Southern Rhodesia (now Zimbabwe).

1912 Morocco is divided into Spanish and French protectorates.

THE MODERN WORLD

Toward the millennium 1900–1990s

At the start of the twentieth century, large areas of the world were controlled by European powers. Britain, France, Belgium, the Netherlands, Portugal, and Spain had built up great empires, while newly united Germany wanted to expand the territory it controlled and this caused the outbreak of World War I in 1914.

Growing unemployment in the 1920s was made worse by the Wall Street Crash in 1929 and the Great Depression that followed. A civil war in Spain from 1936 to 1939 brought the Fascists to power there, while in Germany and Italy Fascist parties were elected to government. In 1939 World War II broke out.

The peace that followed saw great changes in the world. The United States and the Soviet Union emerged as superpowers and the Cold War broke out. As the century draws to a close, and the information revolution gets under way, our world is both smaller and changing faster than ever before.

VOTES FOR WOMEN

In 1848, a women's rights convention in the United States marked the beginning of a movement whose aim was to win voting rights for women everywhere. The movement gained in strength, and in 1890 Wyoming became the first US state to allow women to vote in local elections. In 1893 women voted in national elections in New Zealand.

EMMELINE PANKHURST
Suffragette leader Emmeline Pankhurst was arrested and imprisoned several times for destroying property.

PEACEFUL CAMPAIGNERS
Unlike the militant suffragettes, the suffragists were women who campaigned peacefully for the right to vote. They held rallies to gain support for their cause.

Campaign banner

THE SUFFRAGETTES

In Britain, various women's suffrage (right to vote) societies united in 1897. In 1903 Emmeline Pankhurst set up the Women's Social and Political Union (WSPU), which believed in actions rather than words. It held public demonstrations and attacked property. Its members, known as suffragettes, were often sent to prison. In 1918 the vote was given to all British women over the age of 30. Full voting rights for US women were granted in 1920.

Suffragist sash

Suffragists marched peacefully through the streets.

1893 New Zealand gives women the vote in national elections.

1897 The National Union of Women's Suffrage Societies is formed in Britain.

1902 Australia gives women the right to vote.

1903 Emmeline Pankhurst forms the WSPU.

1913 Suffragette Emily Davison is killed when she throws herself under the king's horse at the Derby.

1917 Russia gives women the vote.

1918 British women over the age of 30 are given the vote. Canadian women are given equal voting rights with men.

1919 Germany, Austria, Poland, and Czechoslovakia give women the vote.

1920 Women in the US are given the vote.

1944 France gives women the vote.

WORLD WAR I

By the late 1800s, Germany had become a major industrial and military power and France and Britain in particular felt threatened by this. Germany formed the Triple Alliance with Austria–Hungary and Italy, while Britain, France, and Russia formed the Triple Entente. Both Britain and Germany enlarged their navies, and all Europe's armies were expanding. In 1914, the assassination by a Serbian citizen of Archduke Franz Ferdinand, heir to the Austro-Hungarian throne, sparked off the war.

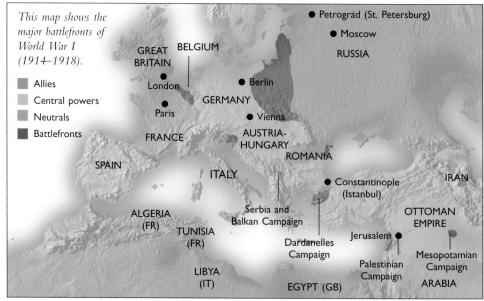

This map shows the major battlefronts of World War I (1914–1918).

- Allies
- Central powers
- Neutrals
- Battlefronts

Petrograd (St. Petersburg)
Moscow
RUSSIA
GREAT BRITAIN
BELGIUM
Berlin
London
GERMANY
Paris
Vienna
FRANCE
AUSTRIA-HUNGARY
ROMANIA
SPAIN
ITALY
Constantinople (Istanbul)
IRAN
ALGERIA (FR)
Serbia and Balkan Campaign
OTTOMAN EMPIRE
TUNISIA (FR)
Dardanelles Campaign
Jerusalem
Mesopotamian Campaign
Palestinian Campaign
LIBYA (IT)
EGYPT (GB)
ARABIA

THE FIRST TANKS
Making their first appearance in battle in 1916, tanks helped to break the stalemate of trench warfare.

THE GREAT WAR

Following the 1914 assassination, Austria–Hungary declared war on Serbia, and Russia mobilized its army to defend Serbia. Germany declared war on Russia and France. Britain joined the war to defend Belgium from German attack. The Great War involved two groups of countries —the Allies (France, Britain, Russia, Italy, Japan, and the United States) and the Central Powers (Germany, Austria–Hungary, and Turkey).

WAR LEADERS
The Allied war leaders led their countries to victory. The United States joined the war in April 1917.

David Lloyd George (Britain)

Woodrow Wilson, President of the United States

Georges Clemenceau (France)

1882 Germany, Austria–Hungary and Italy form the Triple Alliance to defend each other if there is a war.

1891 France and Russia agree that, if either is attacked, the other will give full military support.

1907 Russia joins with Britain and France to form the Triple Entente.

1914 June 28, Archduke Franz Ferdinand is assassinated by a Serbian protester in Sarajevo.

July 28 Austria declares war on Serbia.

August 1 Germany declares war on Russia to defend Austria.

August 3 Germany declares war on France, Russia's ally.

August 4 German armies march through Belgium to France. Britain declares war on Germany. World War I begins.

189

IN THE TRENCHES

Most of World War I was fought from two parallel lines of trenches separated by a short stretch of "no-man's land." This trench warfare was necessary because the power, speed and accuracy of the weapons used on both sides made it impossible to fight a battle in the open. When soldiers did go over the top of their trenches to launch an attack, often only a few yards of ground were gained and the cost in casualties was enormous.

LIFE IN THE TRENCHES
Soldiers slept and ate in their trenches, which were usually cold, muddy, and wet.

Life in the trenches was miserable.

Barbed wire helped to protect the trenches.

Dugouts (underground shelters) offered soldiers some protection from enemy shells and the rain.

*German Fokker
E1 monoplane*

Sopwith Camel

WORLD WAR I PLANES
*At first, planes spied on enemy trenches and troop
movements. Later, they were used in aerial combat and in
bombing raids.*

THE ARMISTICE

In 1917, Russia started peace talks with
Germany. By September 1918 over 1,200,000
well-equipped US soldiers joined the Allied
forces. By October, almost all German-
occupied France and part of Belgium had been
reclaimed, and Turkey and Austria were
defeated. On November 11 Germany and the
Allies signed an armistice, ending World War I.

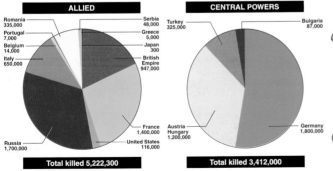

ALLIED

Romania 335,000
Portugal 7,000
Belgium 14,000
Italy 650,000
Russia 1,700,000
Serbia 48,000
Greece 5,000
Japan 300
British Empire 947,000
France 1,400,000
United States 116,000

Total killed 5,222,300

CENTRAL POWERS

Turkey 325,000
Austria Hungary 1,200,000
Bulgaria 87,000
Germany 1,800,000

Total killed 3,412,000

1915 British naval blockade
of Germany leads to a
German submarine
blockade of Britain.

April–May Germany uses
poison gas for first time.

1916 Battle for Verdun,
France, lasts five
months.

July 1 Start of the battle of
the Somme.

1917 US joins the war on
Allied side.

1918 March 3, Russia and
Germany sign armistice.

July Germans launch
offensive on the
Western Front.

August Allies force
Germans to retreat.

October Austria–Hungary
surrenders.

November Armistice is
signed on November 11
at 11 o'clock. World
War I ends.

1919 Treaty of Versailles
orders Germany to pay
large amounts of
compensation to its
former enemies.

191

THE RUSSIAN REVOLUTION

When World War I started, life for most Russians became unbearable. Instead of bringing food and other supplies to the cities, the railroads carried troops to the front. The economy almost collapsed, and in March 1917 riots broke out. Nicholas II abdicated (he and his family were executed in 1918) and a temporary government was established, but unrest continued. The Bolsheviks, led by Lenin, planned a takeover of government. They seized power in November 1917.

STORMING THE WINTER PALACE
Armed workers led by the Bolsheviks stormed the Winter Palace in St. Petersburg in 1917, starting the revolution.

Revolutionary banner

The workers were joined by Russian soldiers, tired of fighting the Germans in World War I.

Bolshevik rioter

СВОБОДА
РАВЕНСТВО
И БРАТСТВО

LEON TROTSKY
(1879–1940)

Trotsky, one of the Bolshevik leaders, was the most powerful man in Russia after Lenin. He was exiled when Stalin came to power, and eventually murdered.

REVOLUTIONARY GOVERNMENT

Lenin's new government made peace with Germany. It broke up the landowners' estates, giving the land to the peasants. Workers took control of the factories. In 1918 civil war broke out, but in 1921 the Bolshevik Red Army defeated the anti-Communist White Russians. In 1924 Lenin was succeeded by Joseph Stalin, an oppressive ruler who killed many of his opponents.

Vladimir Ilyich Lenin

1894 Nicholas II becomes czar.

1898 Russian Social Democratic Workers' Party is founded.

1904–5 Russo-Japanese War.

1905 Around 200,000 people march on the Winter Palace, St. Petersburg. The rebellion is put down, Lenin is exiled.

1917 Lenin returns from exile. Nicholas II abdicates and a republican government is formed. Revolutionaries attack the Winter Palace and the government falls.

1918 Russia withdraws from World War I after signing the Treaty of Brest–Litovsk. The imperial family is executed. Civil war breaks out between the Red Army (Communists) and White Russians (anti-Communists).

1922 The Russian Empire is renamed the Union of Soviet Socialist Republics.

193

TROUBLE IN IRELAND

At the end of World War I, the question of Irish independence from Britain became critical. Most people in the six northern counties, known as Ulster, wanted to remain part of Britain, while in the south most wanted Ireland to become an independent republic. Conflict between the two sides pushed Ireland to the brink of civil war, only prevented by the outbreak of World War I. On Easter Monday, 1916, an armed rebellion declared Ireland a republic. After four days of fighting the protesters surrendered.

THE EASTER RISING
The Easter Rising of 1916 saw fighting on the streets of Dublin between British soldiers and Irish Republicans. Around 100 British soldiers and 450 Irish Republicans and civilians were killed.

Irish Republicans

British soldiers

Barricades were set up in the streets.

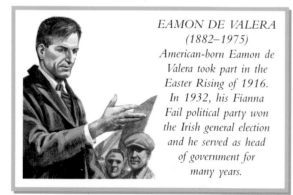

A DIVIDED LAND
After the 1923 settlement, three Ulster counties became part of the Irish Free State; the others remained in the United Kingdom.

THE REPUBLICAN STRUGGLE

In 1918, newly elected Sinn Fein MPs set up their own parliament in Dublin. The Anglo-Irish Treaty of 1921 made most of Ireland independent, leaving Northern Ireland under British rule. Civil war between supporters of the treaty and the Republicans ended when, in 1923, the Republicans accepted the division of Ireland for the time being.

EAMON DE VALERA
(1882–1975)
American-born Eamon de Valera took part in the Easter Rising of 1916. In 1932, his Fianna Fail political party won the Irish general election and he served as head of government for many years.

1886–1893 Attempts to give Ireland its own parliament are defeated.

1896 The Irish Socialist and Republican Party is founded.

1905 Sinn Fein, the Irish nationalist party, is founded.

1912 Outbreak of World War I prevents the enactment of the third Irish Home Rule bill.

1916 Irish Republicans in Dublin in armed revolt against British rule.

1918 Sinn Fein MPs set up their own parliament in Dublin.

1919 Outbreak of fighting between British troops and Irish Republicans.

1921 Anglo-Irish Treaty separates Ulster from the rest of Ireland.

1922 Outbreak of civil war between supporters of the Anglo-Irish Treaty and its opponents.

1937 The Irish Free State becomes Eire.

1949 Eire becomes the Republic of Ireland.

THE GREAT DEPRESSION

After World War I, Germany paid large sums of money to Britain and France as punishment for starting the war, causing its economy to collapse. Other nations also suffered as they paid back money borrowed for their war effort. The money had mostly been borrowed from the United States, where investors pushed up share prices beyond their real value. When prices started to fall, reckless selling made them fall still further, and thousands of investors lost all their money in the Wall Street Crash. It started an economic crisis that threw many people out of work.

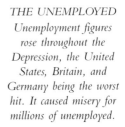

THE UNEMPLOYED
Unemployment figures rose throughout the Depression, the United States, Britain, and Germany being the worst hit. It caused misery for millions of unemployed.

THE WALL STREET CRASH
There was panic in New York in 1929 as investors discovered they had lost all their money.

Many unemployed people became homeless, living in shanty towns of tin and cardboard.

CREATING JOBS
The New Deal introduced by President Roosevelt in 1933 included a program to create more jobs.

THE NEW DEAL

The economic crisis in the United States soon affected the whole world, bringing economic problems and high unemployment to Europe, especially Britain and Germany. In 1933, Franklin D. Roosevelt's government introduced the New Deal, which included protection for people's savings and a construction program to provide jobs.

Soup kitchens serving free food were set up to feed the hungry.

1929 In August, share prices reach a peak. In October, the New York stock exchange on Wall Street crashes as people panic and sell shares.

1932 At the height of the Depression 12 million people in the United States are unemployed. Roosevelt is elected president.

1933 Roosevelt introduces the New Deal. In Germany there are 6 million unemployed.

1935 In Britain 200 men march from Jarrow to London with a petition drawing attention to unemployment.

1939 Around 15 percent of the US workforce is still unemployed.

1941 Full employment returns to the United States as it enters World War II.

197

THE RISE OF FASCISM

Leaders of the Fascist political movement promised to oppose socialism, to restore national pride and to create jobs. In 1922 the Fascists, led by Benito Mussolini as prime minister, replaced Italy's government. From 1925 Mussolini ruled as dictator. In Spain, a terrible civil war broke out in 1936 between the Republicans and the Falangists, led by Francisco Franco. He eventually defeated the Republicans, becoming dictator of Spain in 1939.

Neville Chamberlain, British prime minister from 1937 to 1940.

ADOLF HITLER (1889–1945)
Hitler addressed a huge rally at Nuremberg in 1938. He was a powerful speaker who knew exactly how to win the support of his audience.

The swastika, symbol of the Nazi Party.

*BENITO MUSSOLINI
(1883–1945)*

Mussolini was known as
Il Duce *(The Leader). In
1922 he threatened to
overthrow Italy's
government if he was not
made prime minister. He
impressed many Italians
with his policies at first.*

*General Francisco Franco
(1892–1975)*

THE RISE OF THE NAZIS

In Germany, the Nazi Party and its leader Adolf Hitler rose to power in 1933. The Nazis promised to build Germany into a great state again. Hitler imposed total control on the people, persecuting minorities, especially the Jews. In 1938, Hitler threatened to take over the Sudetenland in Czechoslovakia. To keep the peace, the Sudetenland was given to Germany, but in 1939 Hitler's troops invaded Czechoslovakia and threatened Poland.

1922 Fascists led by Mussolini as prime minister come to power in Italy.

1925 From this date Mussolini rules Italy as dictator.

1931 Spanish monarchy overthrown as Republican party wins the election.

1932 Sir Oswald Mosley forms the British Union of Fascists.

1933 Nazis led by Adolf Hitler come to power in Germany. In Spain, the Falangist (Fascist) Party is created.

1934 Hitler gains total power as his rivals are assassinated.

1936–1939 Spanish Civil War between Republicans and Nationalists (Falangists).

1937 German aircraft bomb the Spanish town of Guernica in support of the Nationalists.

1938 The Anschluss unites Germany and Austria.

1939 Franco becomes dictator of Spain

REVOLUTION IN CHINA

China became a republic in 1911 when the Kuomintang, the Chinese Nationalist Party, overthrew the Manchu Dynasty. When Chiang Kai-shek became Kuomintang leader in 1925, the Chinese Communist Party had already been founded. Civil war broke out between the two parties in 1927.

The Kuomintang claimed to govern the whole of China, but the Communists, under Mao Zedong, established a rival government in Jiangxi province. In 1933 Chiang Kai-shek attacked the Communists. In order to escape, Mao led 100,000 Communists on the "Long March." At its end he became Communist leader.

The Long March from Jiangxi to Shaanxi took 568 days and claimed around 80,000 lives.

About 100,000 marchers set off on the long journey.

The march covered about 6,000 miles.

Mao Zedong led the marchers.

COMMUNIST VICTORY

When the Japanese invaded China in 1937, the Kuomintang and the Communists united to defeat them. But in 1945 civil war broke out again. The Communists defeated the Kuomintang, forcing them off the Chinese mainland and onto the island of Taiwan. On October 1, 1949, mainland China became the People's Republic of China.

Mao Zedong (1893–1976)

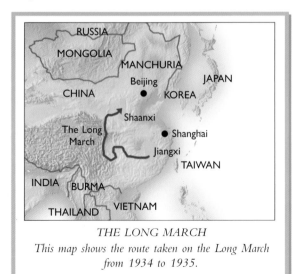

THE LONG MARCH
This map shows the route taken on the Long March from 1934 to 1935.

1905 Sun Yat-sen founds the Kuomintang (Chinese Nationalist Party).

1911 Collapse of the Manchu Empire. Sun Yat-sen becomes president.

1921 Foundation of the Chinese Communist party. Mao Zedong is one of its first members.

1925 Chiang Kai-shek succeeds Sun Yat-sen as leader of China.

1927 Start of civil war between the Communists and the Kuomintang.

1933 Chiang Kai-shek attacks the Communists in Jiangxi.

1934 Mao leads Communists on the "Long March."

1935 Mao becomes leader of the Communist Party.

1937–1945 The Kuomintang and Communists unite to fight against Japan.

1946 Civil war breaks out again.

1949 The People's Republic of China is proclaimed.

201

WORLD WAR II

World War II started on September 3, 1939, two days after Adolf Hitler's troops invaded Poland. The war was fought between the Axis powers (Germany, Italy, and Japan) and the Allies (Britain and the Commonwealth countries, France, the United States, the Soviet Union, and China). The Germans' tactics became known as the *Blitzkrieg* ("lightning war"). They made surprise tank attacks and overcame the opposition quickly. By June 1940, most of Europe had fallen.

AIR RAIDS
The bombing of cities and towns killed and injured many thousands of civilians on both sides.

THE BATTLE OF BRITAIN
The battle of Britain was fought in the skies above southeast England in 1940. Britain had far fewer planes than Germany but managed to win.

THE WAR CONTINUES

In 1940 Hitler's air force, the Luftwaffe, attacked southern England, trying to crush morale and destroy the British air force. The Germans were defeated, preventing Hitler's planned invasion of Britain. Hitler invaded his former ally, the Soviet Union, in June 1941. In December 1941, the United States joined the war following Japan's attack on Pearl Harbor in Hawaii.

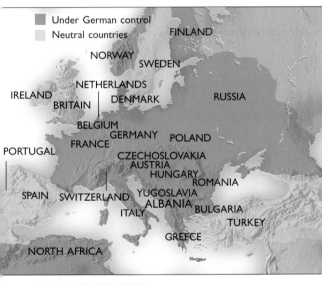

Under German control
Neutral countries

FINLAND
NORWAY
SWEDEN
NETHERLANDS
IRELAND
BRITAIN
DENMARK
RUSSIA
BELGIUM
GERMANY
POLAND
FRANCE
PORTUGAL
CZECHOSLOVAKIA
AUSTRIA
HUNGARY
ROMANIA
SPAIN
SWITZERLAND
YUGOSLAVIA
ALBANIA
ITALY
BULGARIA
TURKEY
GREECE
NORTH AFRICA

GERMAN CONTROL
By the end of 1941 the continent of Europe was almost completely under German control.

1939 Germany annexes Czechoslovakia. Italy annexes Albania. Italian/German alliance.

August 23 Germany and USSR sign non-aggression pact.

August 25 British, French and Polish alliance.

September 1 Germany invades Poland.

September 3 Britain and France declare war on Germany.

September 17 USSR invades Poland.

1940 March USSR takes Finland. German submarines attack British merchant ships.

April–May Germany occupies Norway, Denmark, Belgium, and the Netherlands.

June Germany occupies France. Allies evacuate from Dunkirk.

August–October Battle of Britain.

November Italy tries to invade Greece.

203

THE WORLD AT WAR

By May 1942 Japan had control of Southeast Asia as well as many Pacific islands. By August the US had defeated Japan's navy, stopping them from invading further territory. British troops led by Field-Marshall Montgomery won a decisive battle at El Alamein, Egypt, in 1942. The Allies in North Africa forced the Axis armies to surrender. German troops in the Soviet Union also faced great difficulties. In 1943 the Russians defeated the Germans at the battle of Stalingrad, with many lives lost on both sides.

Field-Marshall Montgomery

Roosevelt and Churchill in Casablanca in 1943.

Hirohito, Emperor of Japan

WAR LEADERS
Montgomery defeated the Germans at El Alamein in 1942. De Gaulle was leader of the resistance movement in France. Roosevelt and Churchill met in 1943 to discuss the war's progress. The Japanese emperor's powers were diminished after Japan's defeat.

Heinrich Himmler, head of the Nazi SS

THE ALLIED INVASION

By July 2, 1944 one million Allied troops had landed in France and were advancing toward Germany. In April 1945 they reached the Ruhr, center of German manufacturing and arms production. Hitler committed suicide in Berlin on April 30. Soviet troops captured Berlin, and on May 7 Germany surrendered.

Charles de Gaulle

THE SIEGE OF LENINGRAD
German and Finnish forces besieged the Soviet city of Leningrad from September 1941 to January 1944.

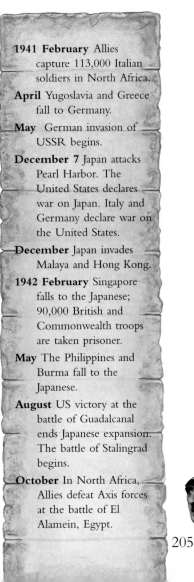

1941 February Allies capture 113,000 Italian soldiers in North Africa.

April Yugoslavia and Greece fall to Germany.

May German invasion of USSR begins.

December 7 Japan attacks Pearl Harbor. The United States declares war on Japan. Italy and Germany declare war on the United States.

December Japan invades Malaya and Hong Kong.

1942 February Singapore falls to the Japanese; 90,000 British and Commonwealth troops are taken prisoner.

May The Philippines and Burma fall to the Japanese.

August US victory at the battle of Guadalcanal ends Japanese expansion. The battle of Stalingrad begins.

October In North Africa, Allies defeat Axis forces at the battle of El Alamein, Egypt.

205

THE WAR ENDS

After the end of the war in Europe, fighting continued in Asia. In September 1944, US troops invaded the Philippines, while the British led a campaign to reconquer Burma. The US dropped an atomic bomb on Hiroshima, in Japan, on August 6, 1945. Three days later a second atomic bomb was dropped on Nagasaki. Thousands of people died, and many thousands more died later from radiation sickness, and other injuries. Five days later, the Japanese government surrendered and on August 14, World War II ended.

ATOMIC BLAST
The atomic bombs that were dropped on Nagasaki (above) and Hiroshima totally devastated the two cities.

D-DAY
The Allied invasion of Europe began on June 6, 1944 (known as D-Day). Around 156,000 troops were landed on the beaches of Normandy, in France, in the largest seaborne attack ever mounted.

Allied soldiers landed on five different beaches in Normandy.

The troops stormed ashore, often under heavy enemy fire.

Landing craft

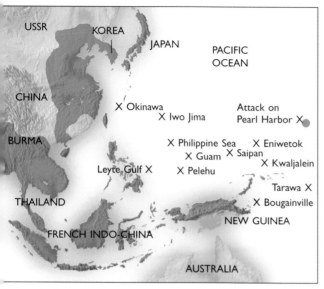

WAR IN THE PACIFIC
By 1942, Japan held all the orange areas on the map.
The crosses mark the ensuing battles in the Pacific.

WAR CASUALTIES

The loss of life from fighting was enormous, and others died through ill treatment as prisoners of war. Millions of civilians died through bombing raids or through illness and starvation. Around six million Jewish people died in concentration camps. After the war, leading Nazis were tried for war crimes and crimes against humanity.

1943 February The Germans are defeated at the battle of Stalingrad.

May Axis troops in North Africa surrender.

July Mussolini is overthrown and Italy declares war on Germany.

1944 June Allied forces land in Normandy, France.

October Allies invade Philippines.

December Start of battle of the Bulge, last German offensive.

1945 February Yalta Conference.

March US forces capture Iwo Jima.

April Hitler commits suicide.

May Soviet troops enter Berlin. Germany surrenders.

July Potsdam Conference agrees division of Germany.

August Japan surrenders after atomic bombs are dropped on Hiroshima and Nagasaki.

INDIAN INDEPENDENCE

The vast colonial territory of India, which included Pakistan and Bangladesh, had been ruled directly from Britain since 1858. But the people of India wanted independence, and in 1885 the Indian National Congress (INC) party was founded to campaign for reforms. Britain saw India as the "jewel in the crown" of its empire and was reluctant to release it. In 1919, British soldiers massacred 400 Indians protesting against British rule. As the campaign for independence grew, Gandhi, leader of the INC, launched a policy of non-cooperation with the British.

DIVIDED INDIA
After the partition of India, millions of people were living in the "wrong" country—Muslims in India and Hindus in Pakistan. Mass migrations followed, during which over one million people were killed.

People piled all their possessions into oxcarts.

People fled on foot or by cart.

WEST PAKISTAN

New Delhi

Karachi

Dhaka

INDIA

BURMA

Rangoon

EAST PAKISTAN

CEYLON

Colombo

THE PARTITION OF INDIA
This map shows how India was divided. Burma (Myanmar) and Ceylon (Sri Lanka) became independent in 1948.

HINDUS AND MUSLIMS

In 1945, India was granted independence. Although the majority of people were Hindus, many Muslims did not want to live under Hindu rule. A separate state for Muslims was agreed, and on August 14, 1947, two areas of northern India became the independent country of Pakistan. The following day the rest of India gained independence.

MOHANDAS GANDHI (1869–1948)
Gandhi was known as Mahatma, meaning "Great Soul." He was a peace-loving man who enjoyed a simple life. After the partition, Gandhi was assassinated by a Hindu extremist.

1885 Indian National Congress (INC) founded.

1905 Foundation of the Muslim League in India.

1919 Government of India Act passed, making some reforms.

1919 Almost 400 Indians are killed by the British army in a massacre at Amritsar.

1920 Gandhi, now leader of the INC, launches non-co-operation with British.

1930 Gandhi leads thousands of protesters on the Salt March.

1934 Mohammed Ali Jinnah becomes president of the Indian Muslim League.

1945 British government grants independence to India.

1947 On August 14, northeast and northwest India become the independent state of Pakistan.

1947 On August 15, the rest of India becomes independent.

209

ISRAEL AND PALESTINE

The ancient city of Jerusalem, spiritual homeland of the Jews, was in a country called Palestine. Most of Palestine's people were Arabs. Britain supported the establishment of a Jewish homeland within Palestine, and in 1922 Britain was asked to rule over Palestine until the country could govern itself. Small numbers of Jews began arriving in Palestine. Following the Nazi persecution of German Jews in the 1930s, the numbers of Jewish immigrants increased. Fighting broke out, and to keep the peace Britain restricted the number of new settlers.

Arab children in Syria, one of the member countries of the Arab League.

The Dome of the Rock

SACRED CITY

The city of Jerusalem is equally sacred to Jews, Muslims and Christians. The Dome of the Rock is sacred to Muslims, while the nearby Wailing Wall (right) is a very important site to Jews.

THE BIRTH OF ISRAEL

After World War II, Palestine was split into a Jewish state and an Arab state, and Jerusalem was made international. The Jews agreed to this, but the Arabs did not. In 1948 the state of Israel was founded. The neighboring Arab countries instantly declared war on Israel but they were quickly defeated.

Israeli soldiers on patrol

GOLDA MEIR (1898–1978)
Golda Meir was prime minister of Israel from 1969 until 1974. Under her leadership, Israel fought the Yom Kippur War of 1973.

DAVID BEN GURION (1886–1973)
Ben Gurion was Israel's first prime minister. Known as the Father of the Nation, he was renowned for his magnetic personality.

1882 First Zionist settlement established in Palestine.

1917 Balfour Declaration supports a Jewish homeland in Palestine.

1922 Britain is given the mandate (permission) to rule over Palestine.

1929 First major conflict between Jews and Arabs.

1930s Persecution of the Jews in Germany.

1939 Britain restricts the number of Jews emigrating to Palestine.

1946 British headquarters in Jerusalem blown up by Zionists (Jewish terrorists).

1947 The United Nations votes to divide Palestine.

1948 On May 14 the state of Israel is founded and the Arab League declares war.

1949 UN negotiates cease-fire.

THE COLD WAR

Although the United States and the Soviet Union were allies in World War II, soon afterwards they became enemies in what was called the Cold War. The Soviet Union set up communist governments in Eastern Europe. To stop communism spreading to the West, the US-backed Marshall Plan gave money to countries whose economies had been ruined by the war. In 1948 the Soviets blockaded West Berlin (the city lay inside Soviet-controlled territory, but was divided between the Allies).

Symbol of the United Nations

The blockade was defeated, and the following year Germany was divided into West and East.

A DIVIDED EUROPE This map shows how Europe was divided after World War II. The boundary between the two halves of Europe was known as the "iron curtain." Few people crossed this divide.

NATO countries
Warsaw Pact
Neutral countries

FINLAND
NORWAY
SWEDEN
NETHERLANDS
DENMARK
RUSSIA
IRELAND
BRITAIN
EAST POLAND
BELGIUM GERMANY
LUXEMBOURG WEST
FRANCE GERMANY CZECHOSLOVAKIA
AUSTRIA
HUNGARY
ROMANIA
PORTUGAL YUGOSLAVIA
SPAIN SWITZERLAND BULGARIA
ITALY ALBANIA
TURKEY
GREECE

Symbol of NATO

NATO

In 1949 the countries of Western Europe and North America formed a military alliance known as the North Atlantic Treaty Organization (NATO).

THE CUBAN CRISIS

Both the United States and the Soviet Union began stockpiling nuclear weapons. In 1962, the Soviet Union built missile bases in Cuba that threatened the United States. The US Navy blockaded Cuba and eventually the Soviets removed the missiles.

Soviet troops

Tanks blocked the streets of Prague.

THE INVASION OF PRAGUE

Soviet tanks entered Prague, Czechoslovakia's capital, in August 1968. A liberal government had introduced many reforms, which worried the Soviets.

1947 US-backed Marshall Plan gives financial aid to European countries.

1948 Blockade of West Berlin by the Soviet Union.

1949 NATO formed. The Soviets explode their first atomic warhead.

1955 Warsaw Pact formed among countries of Eastern Europe.

1956 Soviets invade Hungary to preserve communist rule.

1961 The Berlin Wall is built.

1962 Cuban missile crisis.

1963 The United States and Soviet Union sign Nuclear Test-Ban Treaty.

1964 The United States becomes involved in the Vietnam War.

1968 Soviet Union invades Czechoslovakia to preserve communist rule.

1979 Afghanistan is invaded by the Soviet Union.

1983 The United States invades Grenada.

INTO SPACE

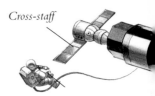

Cross-staff

Soyuz spacecraft

As the Cold War between the superpowers worsened, the "space race" began. Both the US and the Soviet Union wanted to be the first to send a rocket into space. In 1957 the Soviet Union launched *Sputnik 1,* the first artificial satellite to orbit the Earth. The following year the US launched its first satellite *Explorer 1.* In 1969, the US astronaut Neil Armstrong became the first person to walk on the Moon. From the 1970s onward, Britain, China, France, India, and Japan launched their own spacecraft, including weather forecasting or communications satellites.

Astronaut Buzz Aldrin

MEN ON THE MOON
Buzz Aldrin became the second person, after Neil Armstrong, to walk on the Moon on July 21, 1969. The third crew member, Michael Collins, remained aboard Apollo 11's Command Module.

Lunar Module

Solar panels

Antenna

THE MIR SPACE STATION
The Soviet Union launched Mir *in 1986.
Astronauts from the Soviet Union, the
United States and other countries have
visited the space station.*

*Some Russian cosmonauts have
spent over a year on board* Mir.

DEEP INTO SPACE

American and Soviet spacecraft traveled deeper
and deeper into space. They sent back pictures
and other information from planets as far away
as Uranus and Neptune. With the easing of the
Cold War, both sides worked together on
projects, such as building a space station. In
1997 the US spacecraft *Pathfinder* landed a robot
explorer on Mars.

FIRST PERSON IN SPACE
*Cosmonaut Yuri Gagarin of the Soviet
Union orbited the Earth aboard* Vostok 1
for 89 minutes on April 12, 1961.

1957 Soviet Union launches
the first artificial satellite,
Sputnik 1. Laika the dog
is the first animal in
space.

1958 US launches its first
satellite, *Explorer 1.*

1961 Soviets launch first
manned spacecraft,
Vostok 1.

1962 USA launches the first
communications satellite.

1963 Russian cosmonaut
Valentina Tereshkova is
the first woman in space.

1965 Russian cosmonaut
Alexei Leonov becomes
the first person to walk
in space.

1969 US astronaut Neil
Armstrong becomes the
first person to land on
the Moon.

1970 A Soviet spacecraft lands
on Venus.

1971 A Soviet spacecraft lands
on Mars.

1975 Soviet and US
spacecraft link up in
space.

215

AFRICAN INDEPENDENCE

Most overseas colonies in Africa gained their independence in the 1960s and 1970s. Some colonies gained independence peacefully, but others had to use violence. The borders of these newly independent countries did not reflect natural boundaries nor the ethnic groups of the African peoples. This led inevitably to civil wars in countries such as the Congo, Ethiopia, and Nigeria, where people from one area within a country tried to become independent and form a new country of their own.

EUROPE LOSES CONTROL
This map shows the African colonies that gained their independence from Europe. Only Ethiopia and Liberia were never colonized.

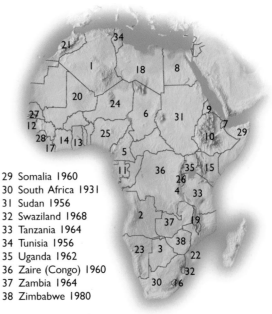

1 Algeria 1962	15 Kenya 1963
2 Angola 1975	16 Lesotho 1966
3 Botswana 1966	17 Liberia
4 Burundi 1962	18 Libya 1951
5 Cameroon 1960	19 Malawi 1964
6 Chad 1960	20 Mali 1960
7 Djibouti 1960	21 Morocco 1956
8 Egypt 1922	22 Mozambique 1975
9 Eritrea 1993	23 Namibia 1990
10 Ethiopia	24 Niger 1960
11 Gabon 1960	25 Nigeria 1960
12 Gambia 1965	26 Rwanda 1962
13 Ghana 1957	27 Senegal 1960
14 Ivory Coast 1960	28 Sierra Leone 1961

29 Somalia 1960
30 South Africa 1931
31 Sudan 1956
32 Swaziland 1968
33 Tanzania 1964
34 Tunisia 1956
35 Uganda 1962
36 Zaire (Congo) 1960
37 Zambia 1964
38 Zimbabwe 1980

Ghanaian chiefs wait for the first session of parliament to begin.

FROM GOLD COAST TO GHANA
Ghana, formerly known as the Gold Coast, gained full independence from Britain in 1957.

CIVIL WARS AND COUPS

Civil wars also broke out in Angola, Rwanda, and Burundi, where rival ethnic groups wanted to control the whole country. In some countries the military overthrew the elected government. Problems also occurred in Algeria, Rhodesia (Zimbabwe), and South Africa, where the white settlers wanted to stay in control.

STRUGGLE IN ZIMBABWE
Robert Mugabe became prime minister of Zimbabwe in 1980. After independence, it took a long and bitter struggle for the black majority to gain power from whites.

1951 Libya gains independence.

1952 Kenyan Mau Mau start independence campaign.

1957 Ghana gains independence.

1960 Zaire gains independence.

1962 Uganda and Algeria gain independence. Eritrea becomes part of Ethiopia.

1963 Kenya becomes independent.

1965 White government of Rhodesia (now Zimbabwe) declares itself independent from Britain.

1969 War breaks out as Biafra seeks independence.

1975 Angola and Mozambique become independent.

1976 Civil war in Angola.

1980 Zimbabwe becomes independent.

1993 Eritrea declares independence from Ethiopia.

1997 Zaire becomes Democratic Republic of the Congo.

STRUGGLE FOR EQUALITY

In the 1950s, many people were still treated unequally because of their race, the color of their skin, their religion, or sex. Black people were especially discriminated against in education, employment, housing, transportation, and health care. With no right to vote, all they could do was protest and campaign. Many nonviolent protests were inspired by Dr. Martin Luther King, a Baptist minister. In 1963 more than 250,000 people marched to Washington, DC, to demand equal justice for everybody. The following year, the US government passed the Civil Rights Act, making discrimination illegal.

MARTIN LUTHER KING (1929–1968)
Martin Luther King's belief in the nonviolent resistance to oppression won him the Nobel peace prize in 1964. In 1968 he was shot dead in Memphis.

Martin Luther King was an outstanding speaker.

218

THE END OF APARTHEID

South Africa's white minority government used Apartheid (separation of whites and blacks) to keep blacks out of power. Peaceful protest ended in 1960 when the police killed 69 unarmed protesters. In 1990 the black leader Nelson Mandela was released after 27 years in prison, and Apartheid was finally abolished.

*NELSON MANDELA
(born 1918)
Mandela's party, the ANC,
won South Africa's first free
elections in April 1994.
Mandela became the country's
first black president.*

*Mandela votes for the
first time in his life.*

1955 Rosa Parks is arrested in Montgomery, Alabama, for refusing to give up her seat on a bus.

1957 Many civil rights groups are brought together by the Southern Christian Leaders Conference, led by Martin Luther King.

1960 South African police fire on anti-Apartheid demonstrators at Sharpeville, killing 69.

1961 Amnesty International is founded to publicize violations of human rights.

1962 Nelson Mandela is arrested and imprisoned for political activities.

1964 The Civil Rights Act is passed in the United States to end all discrimination.

1993 Nelson Mandela and F. W. de Klerk win the Nobel peace prize for their work to end Apartheid.

1995 Fourth World Conference on Women, held in Beijing.

THE VIETNAM WAR

Vietnam, Cambodia, and Laos made up the French colony of Indochina. During World War II Vietnam declared its independence. War broke out between the French and Vietnamese, ending in French defeat in 1954. Vietnam was divided into communist North and noncommunist South, but civil war broke out between the two countries. From 1959, communist guerrillas in the South, known as the Viet Cong, were helped by North Vietnam.

VILLAGE LIFE

Many Vietnamese civilians suffered greatly in the war as their crops and villages were destroyed to flush out and kill the Viet Cong soldiers.

SUPPLY ROUTE
The Viet Cong brought their supplies along the Ho Chi Minh trail, from China through Laos into South Vietnam.

HO CHI MINH (1892–1969)
Ho Chi Minh led Vietnam in its
struggle for independence from France.
Later, he fought for a united Vietnam.

JUNGLE WARFARE

The United States sent
troops to help the South from 1965. In order
to cut off supply lines, US planes bombed
North Vietnam. Villages and jungle areas of
South Vietnam were sprayed with chemicals to
destroy Viet Cong hiding places. In 1969, after
a Viet Cong offensive, the United States began
to withdraw its troops. A cease-fire was agreed
in 1973.

Most Vietnamese were
farmers. They grew rice in the
fields around their villages.

1946 Start of the war
between Vietnamese
nationalists and French
colonial troops.

1954 Vietnamese communists
defeat the French at
Dien Bien Phu. The
country is divided into
North Vietnam and
South Vietnam.

1963 South Vietnamese
government is
overthrown.

1964 War breaks out between
North and South
Vietnam.

1965 US troops arrive in
South Vietnam.

1968 North Vietnamese and
Viet Cong offensive.

1969 25,000 of 540,000 US
troops are withdrawn.

1972 Peace talks start again.

1973 A cease-fire is agreed—
US troops withdraw.

1975 The communists take
control of Vietnam.

1976 Vietnam is reunited
under a communist
government.

CULTURAL REVOLUTION

When Mao Zedong came to power in 1949, many Chinese could not read or write. Many also suffered from ill health and hunger. Mao's government improved health care and provided schools for adults as well as children. Large farms were divided up among the peasants, but there was still not enough food for everyone. In 1958, Mao introduced the Great Leap Forward to make each village self-sufficient in food and other needs. The plan failed, and poor harvests caused even greater food shortages. Many people died of starvation, and in 1959 Mao retired.

BACK TO THE LAND
In the Cultural Revolution schools, universities, factories, and hospitals closed as older people were forced out by radical students. They had to go and work on the land.

MAO TRIUMPHS
A poster from 1949 when Mao first came to power. His initial Five Year Plan improved life for Chinese people.

THE RETURN OF MAO

Mao's successors tried to solve China's economic problems. Mao swept back to power in 1966, launching the Cultural Revolution. Its aim was to overthrow traditional ideas and rid society of people who disagreed with Mao. Young people formed groups of Red Guards and criticized their elders, forcing many out of their jobs. Many people were killed and others were exiled for criticizing Mao. When Mao died in 1976, the Cultural Revolution ended. Mao's successor, Deng Xiaoping, set up trade links and contact with the West.

1949 Mao Zedong's Communist Party takes power.

1953 The Five Year Plan encourages productivity.

1958–1960 The Great Leap Forward results in widespread famine.

1959 Mao Zedong retires.

1960 A split between China and the Soviet Union.

1966 The Cultural Revolution begins. By 1968 factory productivity is 12 percent lower than in 1966.

1973 The "Gang of Four" and Deng Xiaoping argue over Mao's successor.

1974 China tests its first nuclear weapons.

1976 Death of Mao.

1977 Deng Xiaoping comes to power.

1989 Hundreds are killed in Tiananmen Square demonstration.

1997 Death of Den Xiaoping.

MIDDLE EAST CRISIS

An uneasy peace followed Israel's defeat of the Arab League in 1948. Large numbers of Jews continued to migrate to Israel from overseas. The Palestinian Arabs began to campaign for a land of their own. In 1956 Britain and France fought Egypt over control of the Suez Canal. Israel felt threatened and invaded Egypt's Sinai Peninsula, destroying bases there. In the Six Day War in June 1967, Israel took control of all Jerusalem, the West Bank, the Golan Heights, the Gaza Strip, and Sinai. In 1973 Egyptian and Syrian forces attacked Israel but were defeated.

BEIRUT DESTROYED
Large parts of Beirut, the capital of Lebanon, were destroyed by fighting which began in 1976.

THE PEACE PROCESS
At peace talks in 1993, Israeli prime minister Yitzhak Rabin and Yasser Arafat, leader of the Palestinian Liberation Organization, guided by US President Clinton, agreed in principle to limited Palestinian self-rule.

President Clinton

Yasser Arafat

Yitzhak Rabin

AYATOLLAH KHOMEINI
(1900–1989)
Khomeini, a religious leader of Iran, came to power in 1979. He changed Iran into a strictly Muslim state.

WAR AND PEACE

In 1980 war broke out between the oil-producing countries of Iraq and Iran. In 1990 Iraqi troops invaded Kuwait but were defeated by UN forces. Peace agreements have been signed between Israel and Egypt, Jordan, and Syria, but tension and conflict continue to disrupt the peace process.

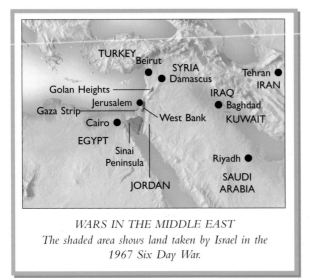

WARS IN THE MIDDLE EAST
The shaded area shows land taken by Israel in the 1967 Six Day War.

1956 Egypt takes control of the Suez Canal.

1964 Formation of the Palestinian Liberation Organization (PLO).

1967 Six Day War, between Israel and Egypt, Jordan and Syria, is won by Israel.

1973 Yom Kippur War between Israel and Egypt and Syria.

1976 Fighting breaks out in Lebanon.

1979 Peace treaty between Israel and Egypt. Islamic republican government is set up in Iran.

1980–1988 Iran–Iraq War.

1982 Israel invades Lebanon.

1990–1991 The Gulf War.

1993 Israeli and Palestinian peace talks.

1994 Israel and Jordan sign a peace agreement.

1995 Israel extends limited self-rule to the Palestinians.

225

THE RISE OF ASIA

Many Asian countries began developing their own industries from the 1950s. With stable governments, modern factories and a well-educated labor force, countries such as Japan, Singapore, South Korea, and Taiwan prospered. The United States helped to rebuild the Japanese economy, which was ruined after Japan's defeat in 1945.

Japanese factories supplied military equipment for the Korean War, helping the economic revival. By the 1970s, Japan was the world's second largest economic power after the United States.

GROWTH AND SUCCESS
Tokyo, capital of Japan, is the center of the Japanese business world. It is one of the world's largest cities. Hong Kong is a major banking, financial and industrial center.

Tokyo

Hong Kong

LOW-PAID WORK
In India, many people work in low-paid manufacturing jobs.

Other industrial nations include Taiwan, Malaysia, and South Korea. They too have well-organized workforces and have invested heavily in computers and other equipment. In the late 1990s, these countries experienced serious economic problems and property values, stocks, and shares fell heavily.

China has modernized its industry, and today has one of the world's fastest growing economies.

1960s Japan starts selling cars on the world market.

1970s Taiwan starts to develop high-technology industries.

1975 Japanese launch the first VHS on to the market.

1976 Japan's exports are more valuable than its imports.

1979 Compact discs are co-developed by a Dutch and a Japanese company.

1980s Japanese become world leaders in the manufacture of motor vehicles.

1995 Over half of China's industrial output comes from privately owned businesses.

1997 Britain returns Hong Kong to Chinese control.

1998 The economies of several Southeast Asian countries experience serious problems.

227

THE COLD WAR FADES

In the early 1960s, the United States and the Soviet Union remained deeply suspicious of each other. Tension between them eased a little with the signing of two agreements to reduce the arms race. However, when Ronald Reagan, an extreme anti-communist, became US president in 1981, he increased military spending. In 1985 the new Soviet leader, Mikhail Gorbachev, introduced reforms, lessening tension between the superpowers. Two years later, Gorbachev and Reagan signed an agreement banning medium-range nuclear missiles.

CZECHS REVOLT
Czechoslovakians demonstrate in the capital Prague in 1989, demanding greater democracy without fear of recriminations.

THE COLLAPSE OF COMMUNISM

Demolishing the Berlin Wall

Gorbachev's reforms led to demands for free elections in Eastern Europe and by the end of 1989, communism had collapsed in Poland, Hungary, East Germany, Czechoslovakia and Romania. In the following year, East and West Germany were reunited for the first time since 1945. In 1991 the Soviet Union was abolished, losing its superpower status. The Cold War had finally ended.

GORBACHEV'S REFORMS
Gorbachev opened the Soviet Union to Western enterprise, encouraging companies such as McDonald's to open up in his country.

1967 The United States, Britain, and the Soviet Union ban the use of nuclear weapons in outer space.

1972 The first Strategic Arms Limitation Talks (SALT) agreement is signed by the US and the Soviet Union.

1979 Second SALT agreement is signed.

1981 Reagan increases US military spending..

1985 Gorbachev makes reforms in the Soviet Union.

1989 Free elections held in Poland. Communism collapses in Hungary, East Germany, Czechoslovakia and Romania. The Berlin Wall is demolished.

1990 East and West Germany are reunited. Free elections are held in Bulgaria.

1991 Albania has a multiparty government. The Soviet Union is replaced by 15 independent nations.

GLOBAL AWARENESS

One of the greatest changes in the twentieth century has been the speed at which information can travel around the world. This revolution in communications, together with faster and more convenient ways of traveling, has helped scientists and others to become aware of what is happening at a global level.

One of the biggest concerns of the late twentieth century has been for the environment. During the 1970s, pressure groups such as Greenpeace were formed to campaign on environmental issues. These concerns included

Recycling is one way in which the Earth's resources may be saved. Paper, glass, metal, and some plastics can be reused again and again.

Carbon dioxide in the air also dissolves in rainwater, making acid rain that can destroy trees and kill fish.

The nuclear reactor at Chernobyl in Ukraine exploded in 1986 releasing radioactive material into the atmosphere.

the dumping of nuclear and toxic waste, the protection of wildlife, and the destruction of rain forests. Scientists began to study the effects of pollution produced by the burning of fossil fuels to power factories and vehicles.

Many governments are now taking action to limit air pollution and encourage people to conserve energy by recycling items such as paper, glass, and metal.

1962 Rachel Carson's *The Silent Spring* creates an awareness of the dangers of pollution.

1972 Government concern for the environment starts when the United States bans DDT, a powerful pesticide.

1976 US scientists voice the first fears about damage to the ozone layer. .

1985 In New Zealand, French agents blow up Greenpeace's ship *Rainbow Warrior*, which is protesting against nuclear testing in the Pacific.

1987 Scientists discover a hole in the ozone layer above the Antarctic.

1992 All nations send representatives to the Earth summit in Rio de Janeiro, Brazil, organized by the UN to discuss the future of the planet.

IMPORTANT BATTLES OF HISTORY

Marathon (490 B.C.) The armies of Athens crushed an attempt by Persia to conquer Greece

Salamis (480 B.C.) Greek ships defeated a larger Persian fleet and thwarted an invasion

Syracuse (414–413 B.C.) During a long war between the city states of Athens and Sparta the Athenians besieged Syracuse but lost power after a heavy defeat

Gaugamela (331 B.C.) Alexander the Great of Macedonia defeated the Persians and conquered the Persian Empire

Metaurus (207 B.C.) A Roman army defeated a Carthaginian attempt to invade Italy

Actium (30 B.C.) A Roman fleet destroyed the Egyptian fleet of Mark Antony and Cleopatra, ending Egypt's threat to Rome

Teutoburg Forest (A.D. 9) German tribes led by Arminius ambushed and destroyed three Roman legions

Châlons (451) Roman legions and their Visigoth allies defeated the Huns, led by Attila

Poitiers (732) The Franks led by Charles Martel defeated a Muslim attempt to conquer western Europe

Hastings (1066) Duke William of Normandy defeated the Saxons under King Harold II and conquered England

Crécy (1346) Edward III of England defeated Philip VI of France, using archers to shoot his opponents

Agincourt (1415) Henry V of England defeated a much larger French army and captured Normandy

Orléans (1429) The French under Joan of Arc raised the siege of Orléans and began liberating France from England

Constantinople (1453) Ottoman Turks captured the city and ended the Byzantine (Eastern Roman) Empire

Lepanto (1571) A Christian fleet defeated a Turkish fleet in the Mediterranean and halted Muslim designs on Europe

Spanish Armada (1588) England fought off a Spanish attempt to invade and conquer it

Naseby (1645) Parliamentary forces defeated Charles I, leading to the end of the English Civil War

Blenheim (1704) During the War of the Spanish Succession, British and Austrian forces stopped a French and Bavarian attempt to capture Vienna

Poltava (1709) Peter the Great of Russia fought off an invasion by Charles XII of Sweden

Plassey (1757) An Anglo-Indian army defeated the Nawab of Bengal, beginning England's domination of India

Quebec (1759) British troops under James Wolfe defeated the French and secured Canada for Britain

Bunker Hill (1775) In the Revolutionary War, British troops drove the Americans from hills near Boston but suffered more casualties

Brandywine Creek (1777) British troops forced American forces to retreat

Saratoga (1777) American troops surrounded a British army and forced it to surrender

Savannah (1778) Britain captured the port of Savannah from the Americans and gained control of Georgia

King's Mountain (1780) Americans surrounded and captured part of a British army

Yorktown (1781) A British army surrendered to a larger American force, ending the Revolutionary War

The Nile (1798) A British fleet shattered a French fleet in Abu Kir Bay, ending Napoleon's attempt to conquer Egypt

Trafalgar (1805) A British fleet defeated a Franco-Spanish fleet, ending Napoleon's hopes of invading England

Austerlitz (1805) Napoleon I of France defeated a combined force of Austrian and Russian soldiers

Leipzig (1813) Austrian, Prussian, Russian, and Swedish armies defeated Napoleon I, leading to his abdication the following year

Waterloo (1815) A British, Belgian, and Dutch army supported by the Prussians defeated Napoleon I, ending his brief return to power in France

Fort Sumter (1861) In the opening battle of the American Civil War, Confederate forces captured this fort in the harbor of Charleston, South Carolina

Merrimack and Monitor (1862) This inconclusive battle was the first between two ironclad warships

Gettysburg (1863) Union forces defeated the Confederates, marking a turning point in the American Civil War

Vicksburg (1863) After a long siege Union forces captured this key city on the Mississippi River

Chickamauga (1863) At this town in Georgia the Confederates won their last major battle

Chattanooga (1863) A few weeks after Chickamauga Union forces won a decisive victory over the Confederates

Tsushima (1905) A Japanese fleet overwhelmed a Russian one, ending the Russo-Japanese War

Tannenberg (1914) At the start of World War I two Russian armies invaded East Prussia, but a German army under Paul von Hindenburg crushed them

Marne (1914) The French and British halted a German invasion of France at the start of World War I

1st Ypres (1914) A series of German attacks on this Belgian town were beaten back with heavy losses on each side

2nd Ypres (1915) The Germans attacked again with heavy shelling and chlorine gas, but gained only a little ground

Isonzo (1916–1917) This was a series of 11 inconclusive battles on the Italo-Austrian front

Verdun (1916) French forces under Philippe Pétain fought off a German attempt to take this strong point

Jutland (1916) This was the major naval battle of World War I; neither Germans nor British won

Brusilov Offensive (1916) A Russian attack led by General Alexei Brusilov nearly knocked Germany's Austrian allies out of the war

Somme (1916) A British and French attack was beaten back by German machine-gunners; total casualties for both sides were more than 1 million

3rd Ypres (1917) British and Canadian troops attacked to drive the Germans back, fighting in heavy rain and mud

Passchendaele (1917) This village was the farthest advance of 3rd Ypres; casualties of both sides totaled 500,000

4th Ypres (1918) This was part of a general German offensive, which died down after heavy fighting

Marne (1918) French, US, and British forces halted the last German attack of World War I

Britain (1940–1941) In World War II, German attempt to eliminate Britain's air force failed

The Atlantic (1940–1944) Germany narrowly lost the submarine war against Allied shipping

Pearl Harbor (1941) In a surprise air attack Japan knocked out much of the United States Pacific fleet at Hawaii

Coral Sea (1942) In the first all-air naval battle, Americans thwarted a Japanese attack on New Guinea

Stalingrad (1942–1943) The German siege of Stalingrad (now Volgograd, Russia) ended with the surrender of a German army of 100,000 men

El Alamein (1942) The British Eighth Army finally drove German and Italian forces out of Egypt

Midway (1942) US fleet defeated a Japanese attempt to capture Midway Island in the Pacific

Normandy (1944) US and British troops landed in occupied France to begin the defeat of Germany; the largest ever seaborne attack

Leyte Gulf (1944) In the biggest naval battle of World War II, a US fleet thwarted a Japanese attempt to prevent the recapture of the Philippines

Ardennes Bulge (1944–1945) A final German attempt to counter the Allied invasion failed

Hiroshima/Nagasaki (1945) Two US atomic bombs on these cities knocked Japan out of World War II

Falklands (1982) A British seaborne assault recaptured the Falkland Islands following an Argentine invasion

Desert Storm (1991) A US, British, and Arab attack ended Iraq's invasion of Kuwait

PRIME MINISTERS OF AUSTRALIA

Name and Party	Held office
Edmund Barton (Protectionist)	1901–1903
Alfred Deakin (Protectionist)	1903–1904
John C. Watson (Labor)	1904
George H. Reid (Free trade)	1904–1905
Alfred Deakin (Protectionist)	1905–1908
Andrew Fisher (Labor)	1908–1909
Alfred Deakin (Fusion)	1909–1910
Andrew Fisher (Labor)	1910–1913
Joseph Cook (Liberal)	1913–1914
Andrew Fisher (Labor)	1914–1915
William H. Hughes (Labor)	1915–1917
William H. Hughes (Nationalist)	1917–1923
Stanley M. Bruce (Nationalist)	1923–1929
James Scullin (Labor)	1929–1932
Joseph A. Lyons (United)	1932–1939
Earle Page (Country)	1939
Robert G. Menzies (United)	1939–1941
Arthur Fadden (Country)	1941
John Curtin (Labor)	1941–1945
Francis M. Forde (Labor)	1945
Ben Chifley (Labor)	1945–1949
Robert G. Menzies (Liberal)	1949–1966
Harold E. Holt (Liberal)	1966–1967

John McEwen (Country)	1967–1968
John G. Gorton (Liberal)	1968–1971
William McMahon (Liberal)	1971–1972
Gough Whitlam (Labor)	1972–1975
Malcolm Fraser (Liberal)	1975–1983
Robert Hawke (Labor)	1983–1991
Paul Keating (Labor)	1991–1996
John Howard	
(Liberal-National coalition)	1996–

Sir Alec Douglas-Home	
(Conservative)	1963–1964
Harold Wilson (Labor)	1964–1970
Edward Heath (Conservative)	1970–1974
Harold Wilson (Labor)	1974–1976
James Callaghan (Labor)	1976–1979
Margaret Thatcher (Conservative)	1979–1990
John Major (Conservative)	1990–1997
Anthony Blair (Labor)	1997–

20TH-CENTURY BRITISH PRIME MINISTERS

Marquess of Salisbury (Conservative)	1895–1902
Arthur Balfour (Conservative)	1902–1905
Sir Henry Campbell-Bannerman	
(Liberal)	1905–1908
Herbert Asquith (Liberal)	1908–1915
Herbert Asquith (Coalition)	1915–1916
David Lloyd-George (Coalition)	1916–1922
Andrew Bonar-Law (Conservative)	1922–1923
Stanley Baldwin (Conservative)	1923–1924
James Ramsay MacDonald (Labor)	1924
Stanley Baldwin (Conservative)	1924–1929
James Ramsay MacDonald (Labor)	1929–1931
James Ramsay MacDonald (Coalition)	1931–1935
Stanley Baldwin (Coalition)	1935–1937
Neville Chamberlain (Coalition)	1937–1940
Winston S. Churchill (Coalition)	1940–1945
Winston S. Churchill (Conservative)	1945
Clement Attlee (Labor)	1945–1951
Sir Winston S. Churchill	
(Conservative)	1951–1955
Sir Anthony Eden (Conservative)	1955–1957
Harold Macmillan (Conservative)	1957–1963

CANADIAN PRIME MINISTERS

Sir John MacDonald (Conservative)	1867–1873
Alexander Mackenzie (Liberal)	1873–1878
Sir John MacDonald (Conservative)	1878–1891
Sir John Abbott (Conservative)	1819–1892
Sir John Thompson (Conservative)	1892–1894
Sir Mackenzie Bowell (Conservative)	1894–1896
Sir Charles Tupper (Conservative)	1896
Sir Wilfred Laurier (Liberal)	1896–1911
Sir Robert L. Borden (Conservative)	1911–1917
Sir Robert L. Borden (Unionist)	1917–1920
Arthur Meighen (Unionist)	1920–1921
W. L. Mackenzie King (Liberal)	1921–1926
Arthur Meighen (Conservative)	1926
W. L. Mackenzie King (Liberal)	1926–1930
Richard B. Bennett (Conservative)	1930–1935
W. L. Mackenzie King (Liberal)	1935–1948
Louis S. St Laurent (Liberal)	1948–1957
John C. Diefenbaker	
(Progressive Conservative)	1957–1963
Lester B. Pearson (Liberal)	1963–1968
Pierre E. Trudeau (Liberal)	1968–1979
Charles J. Clark	
(Progressive Conservative)	1979–1980

Pierre E. Trudeau (Liberal)	1980–1984
John E. Turner (Liberal)	1984
Brian Mulroney (Progressive Conservative)	1984–1994
Kim Campbell (Progressive Conservative)	1994
Jean Chrétien (Liberal)	1994–

PRESIDENTS OF FRANCE SINCE 1947

Fourth Republic

| Vincent Auriol (Socialist) | 1947–1953 |
| René Coty (Republican) | 1953–1958 |

Fifth Republic

Charles de Gaulle (Gaullist)	1959–1969
Georges Pompidou (Gaullist)	1969–1974
Valéry Giscard d'Estaing (Independent Republican)	1974–1981
François Mitterand (Socialist)	1981–1995
Jacques Chirac (Conservative)	1995–

CHANCELLORS OF GERMANY SINCE 1949

(West Germany to 1990, united Germany from then)

Konrad Adenauer (Christian Democratic Union)	1949–1963
Ludwig Erhard (Christian Democratic Union)	1963–1966
Kurt Kiesinger (Christian Democratic Union)	1966–1969
Willy Brandt (Social Democrat)	1969–1974
Helmut Schmidt (Social Democrat)	1974–1982
Helmut Kohl (Christian Democratic Union)	1982–

PRIME MINISTERS OF INDIA SINCE 1950

Jawaharlal Nehru (Congress)	1950–1964
Lal Bahardur Shashtri (Congress)	1964–1966
Indira Gandhi (Congress)	1966–1977
Morarji Desai (Janata)	1977–1979
Indira Gandhi (Congress-I)	1979–1984
Rajiv Gandhi (Congress)	1984–1991
Narasimha Rao (Congress)	1991–1996
Atal Vajpayee (BJP)	1996
Deve Gowda (United Front Coalition)	1996
Inder Kumar Gujral (United Front Coalition)	1996–

NEW ZEALAND PRIME MINISTERS

Richard Seddon (Liberal)	1893–1906
William Hall-Jones (Liberal)	1906
Sir Joseph Ward (Liberal)	1906–1912
Thomas Mackenzie	1912
William F. Massey (Reform)	1912–1925
Francis Bell (Reform)	1925
Gordon Coates (Reform)	1925–1928
Sir Joseph Ward (United)	1928–1930
George Forbes (Coalition)	1930–1935
Michael J. Savage (Labor)	1935–1940
Peter Fraser (Labor)	1940–1949
Sidney J. Holland (National)	1949–1957
Keith Holyoake (National)	1957
Walter Nash (Labor)	1957–1960
Keith Holyoake (National)	1960–1972
Sir John Marshall (National)	1972
Norman Kirk (Labor)	1972–1974
Wallace Rowling (Labor)	1974–1975
Robert Muldoon (National)	1975–1984

David Lange (Labor)	1984–1989
Geoffrey Palmer (Labor)	1989–1990
Michael K. Moore (Labor)	1990
James Bolger (National)	1990–1996
James Bolger (Coalition)	1996–

SOUTH AFRICAN LEADERS

(Prime Ministers up to 1984, thereafter Presidents)

Louis Botha (South African Party)	1910–1919
Jan Smuts (South African Party)	1919–1924
James Hertzog (Pact Coalition)	1924–1939
Jan Smuts (United Party)	1939–1948
Daniel Malan (National)	1948–1954
J. G. Strijdom (National)	1954–1958
D. H. Verwoerd (National)	1958–1966
B. J. Vorster (National)	1966–1978
P. W. Botha (National)	1978–1989
F. W. de Klerk (National)	1989–1994
Nelson Mandela (African National Congress)	1994–

PRESIDENTS OF THE UNITED STATES

George Washington (no party)	1789–1797
John Adams (Federalist)	1797–1801
Thomas Jefferson (Democratic-Republican)	1801–1809
James Madison (Democratic-Republican)	1809–1817
James Monroe (Democratic-Republican)	1817–1825
John Quincy Adams (Democratic-Republican)	1825–1829
Andrew Jackson (Democrat)	1829–1837
Martin Van Buren (Democrat)	1837–1841
William H. Harrison (Whig)	1841

John Tyler (Whig)	1841–1845
James K. Polk (Democrat)	1845–1849
Zachary Taylor (Whig)	1849–1850
Millard Fillmore (Whig)	1850–1853
Franklin Pierce (Democrat)	1853–1857
James Buchanan (Democrat)	1857–1861
Abraham Lincoln (Republican)★	1861–1865
Andrew Johnson (National Union)	1865–1869
Ulysses S. Grant (Republican)	1869–1877
Rutherford B. Hayes (Republican)	1877–1881
James A. Garfield (Republican)★	1881
Chester A. Arthur (Republican)	1881–1885
Grover Cleveland (Democrat)	1885–1889
Benjamin Harrison (Republican)	1889–1893
Grover Cleveland (Democrat)	1893–1897
William McKinley (Republican)★	1897–1901
Theodore Roosevelt (Republican)	1901–1909
William H. Taft (Republican)	1909–1913
Woodrow Wilson (Democrat)	1913–1921
Warren G. Harding (Republican)	1921–1923
Calvin Coolidge (Republican)	1923–1929
Herbert C. Hoover (Republican)	1929–1933
Franklin D. Roosevelt (Democrat)	1933–1945
Harry S. Truman (Democrat)	1945–1953
Dwight D. Eisenhower (Republican)	1953–1961
John F. Kennedy (Democrat)★	1961–1963
Lyndon B. Johnson (Democrat)	1963–1969
Richard M. Nixon (Republican)	1969–1974
Gerald R. Ford (Republican)	1974–1977
Jimmy Carter (Democrat)	1977–1981
Ronald Reagan (Republican)	1981–1989
George Bush (Republican)	1989–1994
William Clinton (Democrat)	1994–

★ Assassinated

	10,000–2000 B.C.	2000–1000 B.C.	1000–500 B.C.	500–200 B.C.
DAILY LIFE	**c. 8000 B.C.** Farming first practiced in Near East and in Southeast Asia **c. 5000 B.C.** Aboriginal Australians begin using boomerangs During this period: copper first used in Asia and N. America	**c. 1500 B.C.** First glass vessels used in Egypt and Mesopotamia **c. 1450 B.C.** Explosion of Thera volcano in Mediterranean wipes out Cretan civilization	**c. 950 B.C.** Poppies are grown in Egypt **c. 900 B.C.** Noble Egyptians and Assyrians begin wearing wigs **776 B.C.** The first Olympic Games are held in Greece	**430–423 B.C.** Plague breaks out in Athens **c. 250 B.C.** Parchment is first made in Pergamum (now Bergama, Turkey) **214 B.C.** The building of the Great Wall of China is started
SCIENCE & TECHNOLOGY	**c. 4000 B.C.** Boats on the river Nile are the first to use sails **c. 3500 B.C.** Sumerians in Mesopotamia invent writing and the wheel **c. 3000 B.C.** Egyptians build irrigation system to water their fields	**c. 2000 B.C.** Tobacco is grown in Mexico and South America **c. 2000 B.C.** Babylonians begin counting in 60s—hence 360° in a circle **c. 1450 B.C.** Ancient Greeks begin using shadow clocks	**c. 1000 B.C.** Phoenicians introduce purple dye made from murex snails **876 B.C.** First known use of a symbol for zero on an inscription in India **c. 700 B.C.** Assyrians begin using water clocks	**c. 500 B.C.** Indian surgeon Susrata performs eye operations for cataracts **c. 500 B.C.** Steel is made in India **406 B.C.** Dionysius of Syracuse, Greece, makes the first war catapult
ARTS & RELIGION	**c. 2800 B.C.** Building begins at Stonehenge in England **c. 2600 B.C.** Work begins on the Great Pyramid in Egypt During this period: Egyptians worship their pharaoh as a god-king	**c. 1500 B.C.** Probable date of the development of the Hindu religion **1339 B.C.** In Egypt, King Tutankhamun is buried with hoard of treasure **c. 1100 B.C.** First Chinese dictionary is compiled	**c. 950 B.C.** Solomon's temple is built in Jerusalem **c. 850 B.C.** Chavin people of Peru make many clay pots and sculptures **c. 563 B.C.** Birth of the Buddha (Siddhartha Gautama) in Nepal	**447–438 B.C.** Greeks build the Parthenon temple in Athens **351 B.C.** Tomb of Mausolus, one of the Seven Wonders of the World, is built **260 B.C.** Emperor Ashoka Maurya makes Buddhism India's state religion

200 B.C.–A.D. 0	A.D. 0–600	A.D. 600–800	A.D. 800–1000
c. 170 B.C. Rome has its first paved streets **c. 50 B.C.** Basic Hindu medical book, the *Ayurveda*, is compiled **46 B.C.** Romans adopt the Julian Calendar and the idea of leap years	**A.D. 79** Vesuvius erupts, destroys Pompeii and Herculaneum **c. A.D. 200** The Chinese invent porcelain **c. A.D. 300** The Maya of Central America invent a calendar	**A.D. 700** Rock-cut temples are begun at Ellora, India **A.D. 750** Hops are first used to make beer in Bavaria, Germany **A.D. 789** Charlemagne introduces his foot as a unit of measurement	**A.D. 812** China issues the earliest paper money **A.D. 851** The crossbow first comes into use in France **A.D. 1000** The Danegeld (a tax to buy off Viking raiders) levied
c. 200 B.C. Gear wheels are invented **c. 110 B.C.** The Chinese invent the horse collar, which is still in use	**c. A.D. 100** Scientist Hero of Alexandria makes the first steam engine **c. A.D. 150** The Chinese make the first paper **A.D. 271** Chinese invent the first form of compass; it points south	**c. A.D. 650** Egyptians invent Greek fire that burns in water **c. A.D. 670** Hindu works on mathematics are translated into Arabic **A.D. 782** In England, Offa's Dyke (a barrier against the Welsh) is started	**c. A.D. 850** Earliest reference in China to gunpowder **c. A.D. 940** Astronomers in China produce a star map **A.D. 984** Canal locks are invented in China
c. 140 B.C. The *Venus of Milo* is carved in Greece **47 B.C.** The great library at Alexandria, Egypt, is destroyed by fire **4 B.C.** Probable birth date of Jesus of Nazareth	**A.D. 30** Probable date of the crucifixion of Jesus of Nazareth **c. A.D. 164** The oldest Maya monuments are built **A.D. 478** First Shinto shrines erected in Japan	**A.D. 622** Arab prophet Muhammad flees from Mecca to Medina **A.D. 650** Art of weaving develops in Byzantium **A.D. 730** Venerable Bede works on his *History of the English Church*	**c. A.D. 850** Building of Great Zimbabwe, now in modern Zimbabwe **A.D. 879** The oldest mosque in Cairo, Ibn Tulun, is built **A.D. 963** First monastery is established at Mount Athos, Greece

	1000–1100	1100–1150	1150–1200	1200–1250
DAILY LIFE	**c. 1009** Persians introduce 7-day week to China, which had 10-day weeks **1086** *Domesday Book* is first complete survey of England **1094** Gondolas come into use in Venice	**1124** Scotland has its first coins **1133** St. Barthlomew's Hospital, London, is founded . **1133** St. Barthlomew's Fair begins in London (closed 1855)	**1151** Game of chess is introduced into England **1189** Silver florins are first minted at Florence, Italy	**1230** Returning Crusaders bring leprosy to Europe **1233** Coal mining at Newcastle, England, begins **1244** First competition for the Dunmow Flitch for married couples is held
SCIENCE & TECHNOLOGY	**1035** Spinning-wheels are in use in China **c. 1050** Chinese begin printing books from movable type **1066** Halley's Comet is seen, and is feared in Europe to portend evil	**1107** Chinese use multicolor printing for paper money **1129** Flying buttresses are first used in building churches in Europe **1142–1154** Books on algebra and optics are translated from Arabic	**1150** The Chinese make the first rockets **1174** Bell tower of Pisa, Italy, is built and at once begins to lean **1189** First European paper mill is built in Hérault, France	**1202** Italian Leonardo Fibonacci introduces 0 (zero) to Europe **1221** Chinese use bombs containing shrapnel
ARTS & RELIGION	**1042** Edward the Confessor begins to build Westminster Abbey **1078** Work begins to build the Tower of London **1098** First Cistercian monastery is founded at Cîteaux, France	**1110** Earliest known miracle play is performed in England **1119** Military Order of Knights Templars is founded **1123** First Lateran Council in Rome forbids priests to marry	**1151** Golden age of Buddhist art in Burma (now Myanmar) **1155** Carmelite Order of monks is founded in Palestine **1170** Archbishop Thomas à Becket is murdered in Canterbury Cathedral	**1215** Spanish priest Dominic founds the Dominican Order **c. 1220** Italian poets develop the form of the sonnet **1229** The Inquisition in Toulouse, France, forbids laymen to read the Bible

1250–1300	1300–1350	1350–1450	1450–1500
1278 In London, 278 Jews are hanged for clipping coins **1284** Legend of the Pied Piper of Hamelin begins; it may be founded on fact	**1332** Bubonic plague is first heard of in India **1347–1351** The Black Death (bubonic plague) kills 75 million Europeans **1348** Edward III of England founds the Order of the Garter	**1360** France issues its first francs **1416** Dutch fishermen begin using drift nets **1433** Holy Roman emperors adopt the double-eagle as an emblem	**1467** Scots parliament bans football and golf **1485** Yeomen of the Guard formed in England **1489** The symbols + and − come into general use
1267 English scientist Roger Bacon proposes the use of spectacles **c. 1290** Cable bridges are built over deep valleys in the Andes **1299** Florence, Italy, bans the use of Arabic numerals	**c. 1310** First mechanical clocks are made in Europe **1327** Grand Canal in China, begun A.D. 70, is completed **1336** University of Paris insists that students study mathematics	**c. 1380** Cast iron becomes generally used in Europe **1408** The Dutch use a windmill for pumping water **c. 1440** Johannes Gutenberg of Germany begins printing with type	**1454** Gutenberg produces the first printed Bible **1476** William Caxton prints the first book in English **1480** Italian artist Leonardo da Vinci designs a parachute
1256 Order of Augustine Hermits, or Austin Friars, founded **1257** Persian poet Saadi writes *The Fruit Garden* **1285** French composer Adam de la Halle writes comic opera *Le Jeu de Robin et de Marion*	**1325** Aztecs of Mexico build their capital city, Tenochtitlan **1348** Italian poet Giovanni Boccaccio begins writing the *Decameron* (to 1353) **1349** Persecution of Jews breaks out in Germany	**1375** First appearance of Robin Hood in English legends **1387–1400** Chaucer writes *The Canterbury Tales* **1417** End of the Great Schism (between the pope in Rome and the pope in France)	**1453** St. Sophia Basilica, Constantinople, becomes a mosque **1473** Sheet music printed from wood blocks is produced in Germany **1484** Papal bull is issued against sorcery and witchcraft

	1500–1525	1525–1550	1550–1575	1575–1600
DAILY LIFE	**1504** First shillings are minted in England **1517** The first coffee is imported into Europe **1519** Hernando Cortés reintroduces horses to North America	**1525** Hops are introduced to England from France **1528** Severe outbreak of bubonic plague hits England **1531** Halley's Comet returns, causing great alarm	**1550** People begin playing billiards in Italy **1565** The first potatoes arrive in Spain from America **1568** Bottled beer is first produced in London	**1582** Most Roman Catholic countries adopt new Gregorian calendar **1596** Tomatoes are introduced into Europe from America **1596** Sir John Harington of England invents the first water closet (lavatory)
SCIENCE & TECHNOLOGY	**1502** Peter Henlein of Germany makes the first pocket watch **1507** The name America is used on maps for the first time **1520** First turkeys are imported to Europe from North America	**1528** Michelangelo designs fortifications for the city of Florence, Italy **1530** Swiss physician Paracelsus writes book on medicine **1543** Nicolas Copernicus declares that the Earth revolves around the Sun	**1557** Julius Scaliger of Italy discovers the metal platinum **1569** Gerhardus Mercator invents his projection for maps **1570** The camera obscura, or pinhole camera, is invented	**1576** Danish astronomer Tycho Brahe begins sensational discoveries **1589** William Lee in England invents a knitting machine **1592** Galileo of Italy invents a primitive thermometer
ARTS & RELIGION	**1503** Leonardo da Vinci paints the *Mona Lisa* **1508–1512** Michelangelo paints the ceiling of the Sistine Chapel, Rome **1517** Martin Luther begins the Reformation in Europe	**1534** English Church breaks from Rome, with the monarch as its head **1534** Ignatius Loyola of Spain founds the Jesuit order **1545** First ever book fair is held in Leipzig, Germany	**1560** Scotland breaks with the Roman Catholic Church **1570** Andrea Palladio writes influential work on architecture **1572** Massacre of St. Bartholomew: many French Protestants are killed	**1576** First theater in England opens in London **1590–1592** Three popes die in a period of three months **1590–1594** William Shakespeare of England begins writing his plays

1600–1625	1625–1650	1650–1675	1675–1700
1607 Table forks come into use in England and France **1610** The first China tea is imported into Europe by the Dutch **1619** First black slaves are employed in Virginia	**1626** The Dutch buy Manhattan Island from Native Americans for $24 **1630** The card game cribbage is invented **1650** England has its first coffee house (in Oxford) and starts drinking tea	**1658** Sweden's state bank issues the first banknotes in Europe **1665** Plague ravages London, killing 68,596 people **1666** Fire destroys most of London and ends the plague there	**1677** Ice cream becomes popular in Paris **1683** Wild boars become extinct in Britain **1697** Fire destroys most of the Palace of Whitehall, London
1608 Dutchman Hans Lippershey invents the microscope **1613** Galileo agrees with the theory that the Earth goes round the Sun **1622** William Oughtred, English mathematician, invents the slide rule	**1642** Blaise Pascal of France designs an adding machine **1642** Evangelista Torricelli of Italy invents the barometer **1650** Otto von Guericke of Germany invents an air pump	**1662** Work begins on Louis XIV's Palace of Versailles in France **1665** Isaac Newton of England develops calculus **1675** Greenwich Royal Observatory is founded in England	**1682** Edmund Halley of England observes comet now named after him **1684** Robert Hooke of England invents the heliograph **1698** Thomas Savery of England invents the first steam pump
1605 Miguel de Cevantes of Spain writes the first part of *Don Quixote* **1611** Royal mosque at Isfahan, Persia (Iran) is built **1611** The Authorized Version of the Bible is published in Britain	**1642** Rembrandt van Rijn of the Netherlands paints *The Night Watch* **1645** Presbyterianism is made England's official religion **1648** George Fox founds the Society of Friends (Quakers)	**1650** Archbishop James Ussher of Ireland says the Creation was in 4004 B.C. **1662** England forbids Nonconformist priests to preach **1667** The colonnaded square of St. Peter's, Rome, is completed	**1677** John Dryden is England's leading poet **1678–1684** John Bunyan of England writes *The Pilgrim's Progress* **1692** At witch trials in Salem, Massachusetts, 19 people are hanged

	1700–1725	1725–1750	1750–1775	1775–1800
DAILY LIFE	**1712** Last execution of a witch in England takes place **1722** Thomas Guy helps found Guy's Hospital, London **1725** New York City gets its first newspaper, the *New York Gazette*	**1727** Brazil sets up its first coffee plantation **1732** Benjamin Franklin publishes first *Poor Richard's Almanac* **1742** Anders Celsius of Sweden invents the centigrade thermometer	**1752** Britain adopts Gregorian calendar, dropping 11 days **1755** Earthquake kills 30,000 people in Lisbon **1768** Publication of the *Encyclopaedia Britannica* in weekly parts begins	**1779** First running of the Derby horse race at Epsom, England **1787** United States ADopts the Stars and Stripes flag **1792** Denmark abolishes the slave trade
SCIENCE & TECHNOLOGY	**1707** Johann Böttger of Germany discovers how to make hard porcelain **1709** Abraham Darby of England uses coke to smelt iron **1714** Gabriel Fahrenheit makes a mercury thermometer	**1733** John Kay of Britain invents the flying shuttle **1735** John Harrison of Britain builds first accurate chronometer **1737** Georg Brandt of Sweden discovers cobalt	**1751** Carl Linnaeus of Sweden publishes his book on botany **1769** James Watt of Scotland invents the steam condenser **1773** First cast iron bridge built at Coalbrookdale, England	**1783** Montgolfier brothers of France make first hot-air balloon ascent **1792** Claude Chappe of France invents the mechanical semaphore **1793** Eli Whitney of the United States invents the cotton gin
ARTS & RELIGION	**1709** Bartolommeo Cristofori of Italy invents the piano **1710** Building of St. Paul's Cathedral in London is completed **1716** Chinese emperor bans the teaching of Christianity	**1730** John and Charles Wesley begin Methodist movement **1735** Imperial ballet school opens in St. Petersburg, Russia **1741** German George Frederick Handel composes *Messiah* in England	**1751–1772** French scholars compile the *Encyclopédie* **1767** Jesuits are expelled from Spain **1768** The Royal Academy of Arts is founded in London	**1778** In Milan, Italy, La Scala Opera House opens **1790** Jews in France are granted civil liberties **1793** Building of the Capitol in Washington, DC, begins

1800–1825	1825–1850	1850–1875	1875–1900
1807 Britain ends the slave trade **1815** Tambora Volcano in Indonesia erupts: 50,000 people are killed **1819** Freedom of the press is guaranteed in France	**1840** Penny Postage and adhesive stamps are introduced **1841** First pioneer wagon train leaves Missouri for California **1844** First co-operative society is formed in Rochdale, England	**1864** Louis Pasteur of France invents pasteurization **1867** United States buys Alaska from Russia for $7.2 million **1874** Walter Wingfield invents Sphairistiké— now called lawn tennis	**1879** F.W. Woolworth opens his first five-and-ten store in Utica, NY **1890** Ellis Island opens as US immigration center **1900** US troops help suppress "Boxers" in Beijing
1814 George Stephenson builds first successful steam locomotive **1815** Humphrey Davey invents the miners' safety lamp **1816** Réné Laennec of France invents the stethoscope	**1827** Joseph Niépce of France takes world's first photograph **1844** Samuel Morse demonstrates the use of the Morse Code **1847** James Simpson of Britain uses chloroform as an anesthetic	**1860** Christopher Scholes of the US invents a practical typewriter **1872** *HMS Challenger* begins a world survey of the oceans **1873** Joseph Glidden of the US invents barbed wire	**1876** Alexander Graham Bell invents the telephone **1885** Karl Benz of Germany builds the first automobile **1895** Guglielmo Marconi of Italy invents wireless telegraphy
1808 Napoleon abolishes the Inquisition in Italy and Spain **1814** Walter Scott writes his first novel, *Waverley* **1822** Royal Academy of Music is founded in London	**1830** Joseph Smith founds the Church of Latter-Day Saints (Mormons) **1835** Hans Christian Andersen publishes his first fairy tales **1846** Adolphe Sax of Belgium invents the saxophone	**1865** William Booth founds the Salvation Army in Britain **1868** Louisa M. Alcott writes *Little Women* **1874** Impressionist movement in painting starts in Paris	**1879** Mary Baker Eddy founds Christian Science Church **1884** Mark Twain writes *Huckleberry Finn* **1896** Theodor Herzl of Austria proposes a Jewish state in Palestine

	1900–1915	1915–1930	1930–1945	1945–1960
DAILY LIFE	**1903** The first teddy bears are made in Germany **1906** An earthquake destroys most of San Francisco **1912** Liner *Titanic* sinks on maiden voyage; more than 1,500 people drowned	**1918** British women over the age of 30 gain the vote **1918** First airmail service is established in the United States **1929** Wall Street crash: biggest world economic crisis begins	**1936** King Edward VIII abdicates to marry Wallis Simpson **1938** Orson Welles's *War of the Worlds* causes panic **1945** Bebop form of jazz comes into fashion	**1953** Mount Everest is climbed for the first time **1954** Roger Bannister runs the mile in under four minutes **1958** First life peerages are created in Britain
SCIENCE & TECHNOLOGY	**1903** The Wright Brothers make the first powered flights **1907** Louis Lumière of France develops color photography **1909** Louis Blériot of France flies across the English Channel	**1917** Ernest Rutherford of Britain splits the atom **1925** John Logie Baird invents a primitive form of television **1928** Alexander Fleming accidentally discovers penicillin	**1935** Radar is developed for use in detecting aircraft **1937** Frank Whittle builds the first jet aero engine **1940** Howard Florey develops penicillin as a working antibiotic	**1946** ENIAC, first fully electronic digital computer, is built **1956** Albert Sabin invents oral vaccine against polio **1957** Soviet Union launches the first Earth satellites, *Sputniks 1* and *2*
ARTS & RELIGION	**1901** Ragtime music becomes popular in America **1909** Sergei Diaghilev's Ballets Russes starts performing in Paris **1909** First Jewish kibbutz is founded in Palestine	**1916** Artists start Dadaist movement in Switzerland **1917** Balfour Declaration: Britain backs homeland for Jews in Palestine **1924** Mahatma Gandhi fasts in protest at religious feuding	**1932** Methodist Churches in Britain reunite after 135 years **1935** American George Gershwin writes *Porgy and Bess* **1937** First full-length cartoon film, *Snow White and the Seven Dwarfs*	**1947** *The Diary of Anne Frank* is published **1947** The Dead Sea Scrolls are discovered in caves at Qumran, Jordan **1950s** Rock and Roll develops

1960–1970	1970–1980	1980–1990	1990–2000
1966 Miniskirts come into fashion **1967** Francis Chichester completes single-handed voyage around the world **1970** Storms and floods kill 500,000 people in East Pakistan (Bangladesh)	**1974** Richard Nixon resigns as US president **1976** Earthquakes in Guatemala, China, Italy, the Philippines, Indonesia, and Turkey: 780,000 people die **1980** Smallpox is eradicated worldwide	**1982** Mt. St. Helens volcanic eruption kills 60, causes $3 billion damage in Washington State **1987** World stock market crash on Black Monday **1989** World ban on ivory trading imposed	**1994** Channel Tunnel is completed at a cost of £10 billion **1998** Hurricane Mitch devastates Central America **1999** President Bill Clinton acquitted in impeachment trial
1963 Theory of continental drift is proved by two Britons **1967** Christiaan Barnard performs first human heart transplant **1969** Neil Armstrong, Buzz Aldrin walk on moon	**1971** Space probes orbit Mars and send back photographs **1972** *Apollo 17* crew make last manned visit to the Moon **1978** Louise Brown, the first "test tube baby," is born	**1984** The first Apple Macintosh micro-computer goes on sale **1986** The Dutch complete their flood protection scheme after 33 years **1988** New undersea tunnel links Honshu and Hokkaido, Japan	**1993** Astronauts repair the Hubble Space Telescope **1993** Two Britons complete the first foot crossing of Antarctica **1997** US robot, controlled from Earth, explores surface of Mars
1966 New Metropolitan Opera House opens in New York City **1968** Four Soviet writers are jailed for "dissidence" **1968** In Northern Ireland, Catholics and Protestants clash	**1971** *Fiddler on the Roof* closes after run of 3,242 performances **1978** Popes Paul VI and John Paul I die; John II becomes first non-Italian pope for 456 years **1980** John Lennon is murdered in USA	**1985** Live Aid concert raises $60 million for African famine relief **1986** Wole Soyinka is first black African to win the Nobel Prize for Literature **1986** Desmond Tutu beomes archbishop of Cape Town	**1992** Ten women become Anglican priests in Australia **1993** Missing treasure from Troy (found in 1873) is rediscovered in Russia **1996** Strict Islamic law is imposed in Afghanistan

INDEX

ACKNOWLEDGMENTS

The publishers wish to thank the following artists who have contributed to this book.

Martin Camm, Richard Hook, Rob Jakeway, John James, Shane Marsh, Roger Payne, Mark Peppé, Eric Rowe, Peter Sarson, Roger Smith, Michael Welply and Michael White.

PHOTO CREDITS
Page 9 (TR) Giraudon/Bridgeman Art Library; page 14 (BL) AKG London; page 66 (BL) AKG London; page 42 (C) AKG London; page 116 (C) AKG London; page 170 (C) ET Archive.

All other photographs from the Miles Kelly Archive.